A twenty-year veteran of the financial services industry, an attorney, and president of his own North Carolina–based advisory firm, Wealth Capital Group, for almost a decade now DANIEL TAYLOR has been spreading his empowering message of how to "be your own advisor" in the areas of conflict resolution and financial planning.

Taylor's trademarked Divorce Mediation Program, a tool for reducing the time, complexity, and costs associated with divorce, is recognized and used internationally by everyone from lawyers and business professionals to folks like you and me (more than 70 percent of them women).

His highly successful Parent Care Solution is an extension of that work. The powerful program is aimed at helping professionals in the elder care, long-term care, financial planning, estate planning, insurance, and nursing home industries nationwide deal more sensitively, more efficiently, and more effectively with family members in crisis as our population ages. It was born of his own experience when suddenly confronted with the emotional, practical, and financial challenge of caring for an aging parent, a dilemma that confronts millions of Americans every day.

The Parent Care Conversation is a major step forward in spreading the message and methods of Taylor's Parent Care Solution on a personal level to a broad audience of consumers as well as to business and social services professionals faced with this growing and sometimes devastating issue.

A native of West Virginia, Taylor graduated with honors from West Virginia University College of Law in 1983, after serving in the U.S. Air Force and completing Navy Officer Candidate School. Following law school, he entered the financial services industry, where he was instrumental in designing and implementing the executive financial planning department at what is now the headquarters of Bank of America.

Prior to opening his own firm, Taylor became affiliated with the nationally known and highly acclaimed Strategic Coach program, where he has served as mentor and coach to more than three thousand business entrepreneurs in more than sixty industries throughout the United States, Canada, Europe, and Australia.

Taylor's charismatic delivery style, his knowledge, and his passion for the issues closest to him, such as planning more effectively for the long-term care of aging parents and other family members as our global population ages, have made him a much sought-after keynote speaker and motivator. Over the past five years, he has delivered more than fifty major keynote addresses on the financial and legal aspects of this critical health care topic to such high-profile organizations as Metropolitan Life, Legal and General Insurance of Australia, MacKenzie Financial, Financial of Canada, Lincoln Financial Services, and H.D. Vest. He has also conducted more than 250 workshops on this and related topics for financial advisors worldwide.

Taylor lives and works in Charlotte, North Carolina, with his life partner, Christine Sheffield, her daughter, Ashley, and their two cats and three dogs.

To my father, Clyde J. Taylor

CONTENTS

Part Three: Implementing Parent Care Decisions

The Parent Care Conversation

No Family Left Behind

A Living Nightmare

Let me tell you about Joshua, a fifty-eight-year-old corporate executive who lives in Bethesda, Maryland, with his fifty-seven-year-old wife Ann. They have a daughter who is a senior in a private school and a son who is attending the University of Maryland. Both Joshua and Ann also have parents who are in various stages of elder care.

Ann's folks, both of them in their seventies, live in a West Virginia retirement village they "sort of like." She visits them every other week, making the round-trip in just about four hours—in time for her to be home when her daughter gets out of school. She goes during the week so she can help Joshua out with his aging parents on weekends.

Joshua's seventy-eight-year-old dad lives in the addition they built onto their home in Bethesda, where he moved after Joshua's mom, also in her seventies and suffering from Alzheimer's disease, went into a nursing home. The nursing home is about forty-five minutes away. Ann drives Joshua's dad there to visit at least twice during the week and once on weekends. Sometimes Joshua will accompany her if he isn't away on company business.

As a senior vice president, Joshua is responsible for $50 million a year in revenue and forty-five salespeople who work in his division. He leaves for work at six thirty in the morning and often arrives home after seven in the evening. Part of each Saturday morning is spent catching up on e-mail and planning the next week's activities. At least once a month he and Ann are involved in a weekend company function, hosting salespeople, suppliers, and vendors or entertaining key accounts to maintain business relationships.

Joshua also spends an increasing amount of time each day talking to his father on the phone and consoling him. He fears that his father is slipping into depression but feels powerless to do anything about it; given his limited free time during the week, he simply cannot afford to spend more than just a few minutes a day checking in on his dad, and suffers guilt about it. Joshua and Ann's daughter loves her grandfather, but she is a busy senior with lots of activities and the demands of endless amounts of homework required to get the grades she needs to be accepted at the colleges she is considering. When she is home, her grandfather always wants to chat, ask her about her day, and reminisce. She has taken to staying at her friend's house after school just to have some privacy. She secretly wishes her grandfather would go to "the home" with her grandmother so that they could all have their lives back again, and is guilty about her feelings. Meanwhile, most days Ann doesn't know whether she's coming or going. Caught, between her parents and Joshua's, in an endless cycle of caregiving, trying to be a mom, and keeping up the corporate spouse duties that Joshua's position requires, she has absolutely no time for relaxation, reflection, or respite.

Adding to the emotional stress is financial pressure, since both sets of parents are virtually broke, having exhausted much of their assets to pay for their current care regimen. Joshua and Ann help out with a monthly subsidy of $2,700 and supply their folks with extra clothing and gifts during the year as well. That's the tangible cost. The intangible costs to Joshua and Ann of driving time, reduced energy, increased stress, sleepless nights, and related health problems are almost impossible to calculate.

Joshua has been dipping into his 401(k) at work to help out with the situation and keeping this a secret from his wife. The raise he was hoping for didn't come through, and he doesn't want Ann to be worried about money. He has set up an equity line of credit on their house as a backup and has the monthly statements sent to his office so Ann will not be alarmed by seeing them. He also has not told her that this is a do-or-die year for his division. If the division doesn't make its numbers, he and everyone else will be looking for another job. That scares the hell out of him. He can't even imagine how he will find one at his age, just seven years away from retirement. He's told the kids to take out loans for college, and he will pay them off after they graduate, but deep inside he knows he's reaching.

Just at the time of their lives when they thought they would be able to slow down and relax a bit, Joshua and Ann find themselves working harder than ever, watching their savings dwindle, and feeling their life go emotionally, physically, and financially out of control.

All Too Common

Nightmare scenarios like this are not rare these days. In fact, they are all too common. They have become the norm rather than the exception and are only growing more widespread as America's graying population explodes in size. Reports *USA Today:* "Studies show that [adult children] providing the highest level of care [for aging parents]—40 hours a week and more—are stressed, develop health problems and often don't have ways to cope. In fact, 46 percent of those providing the highest level of care rate their physical strain 4 or 5 on a 5-point scale; 63 percent rate emotional stress 4 or 5; and 34 percent rate their financial burden as 4 or 5."

Nevertheless, long-term care for our parents remains a huge but neglected issue, especially on the home front. Most parents and their kids avoid talking about it. They put off having this important discussion or ignore it altogether, thinking they'll get by, but then suddenly something happens—a catastrophic event or prolonged illness—and everybody must scramble to figure things out under the worst possible conditions, at the worst possible time.

So many questions need answering: What's the best thing to do? How to do it? Where to turn? How much will it cost? Where will the money come from? And more questions keep piling up, each of them underscored by the financial realities at stake. Worse even than the financial crisis this can lead to is the relationship crisis that often follows in its wake between parents and children, siblings, and other family members, causing wounds that may never heal.

My Story

No parent wants to be a burden on his or her children, but very often that is exactly the result of ignoring the parent care issue. Rather than protecting them, parents unwittingly make their children and grandchildren the recipients of tremendous financial and emotional burdens.

I know this from my own experience with my own dad.

On a spring Sunday, in April 2000, I received a strange phone call concerning my father. On the other end of the phone was a friend of our family who relayed to me that my father was in protective custody of the police in Danville, Virginia, a small town about a hundred miles north of his home in Winston-Salem, North Carolina. The police had stopped him for driving erratically at four thirty in the morning. By their account, he was disoriented and confused, and from all reports had been driving throughout the night.

When I finally arrived a day later, he seemed a bit nonchalant about the entire matter—as if he had forgotten to shut the kitchen door or perhaps left a light on in the car. Little did I know that the reason for this casualness was that in his mind nothing had happened worth remembering—in fact, he didn't even recall the incident. The only thing he thought strange was that it was Tuesday now, and his son almost never came to see him on Tuesday.

On Thursday, we drove together to Baptist Hospital in Winston-Salem for an appointment with a gerontologist. I was grateful that day for the physician's assessment and remain so to this day. Although, if I had known what the next five years were going to bring, I may have been less amazed and more concerned.

During the nearly four-hour assessment, my father was given a battery of mental, neuropsychological, physical, and emotional evaluations designed to pinpoint the cause of his rather bizarre behavior.

After what seemed an endless afternoon in the waiting room, the young doctor came out and asked if he could speak with me. He introduced himself with all the calmness that physicians, clergy, and prison wardens exhibit when the news they have is not the news you want to hear, nor could ever imagine.

It seems my father was suffering from late-stage dementia (he had been progressively forgetful for almost five years) and was, in fact, in the early stages of Alzheimer's disease. The doctor explained what had happened with the driving incident. Dad had simply turned left instead of right, or perhaps forgot where he was going, and simply kept driving as if that is what he had intended to do in the first place.

The doctor continued for the next fifteen minutes or so, explaining all the signs and symptoms of Alzheimer's, the progression of the disease, and the realistic outcome the family could expect. In retrospect, I listened with the sort of numbness that a ballplayer might feel listening to his coach send him back to the huddle with a play when two minutes before he had been clotheslined by someone twice his size.

In his closing words, he said, "Your father is fine, but he cannot live alone or drive alone again." In my numbed naivety I asked, "From what point?" The young doctor, with all the patience of one who deals with the mentally ill on a daily basis, replied, "Why, from right now."

That afternoon, on the Thursday before Palm Sunday in the year 2000, the intergenerational transfer of power, wealth, and influence in the Taylor family of Winston-Salem, North Carolina, took place. My father became my child, and I became his parent.

The next five days were a blur of action, reaction, shock, anger, denial, disbelief, depression, rage, elation, sadness, pain, and fatigue. Looking back, I'm not sure how we made it through those five days without permanently damaging everything we held dear.

I phoned my companion of nine years, Christine, to tell her that I was bringing my dad home for a few days until we could sort things out, and that she should let her fourteen-year-old daughter, Ashley, know that I was coming, as well as our two dogs, two cats, and whoever else happened to be in our home at the time.

Our home in Charlotte is a 4,200-square-foot, three-story stucco house with a swimming pool, lots of stairs, original art, and nothing at all to make a seventy-four-year-old retired railroad foreman feel comfortable. At the time, I had no idea that the interior design deficiencies would be the least of our concern.

When we arrived, I helped my father downstairs to the combination library, home theater, doggy domicile, and entrance to the pool that is otherwise known as the basement of our house. Most of that Thursday was spent making small talk, fixing assorted meals, and, when my dad couldn't see me, sneaking into Chris's office to cry about the entire situation. I lost count of the visits I made to that office over the weekend.

That night I had to bathe, dress, shave, and generally get my father ready for bed. Any modesty, on either of our parts, was quickly dispensed with, since we both intuitively knew what I had to do. He had to let me do what he could no longer do or remember to do for himself. I slept with the proverbial one eye open as I listened for him to get up, miss the bathroom, and trip down the stairs to be impaled on a blown-glass flower in the hallway. When morning finally came, I began what was to become the ritual for the next few days: newspaper small talk, coffee, two eggs and bacon, and assisting with his bowel movement. It was the beginning of a day of news, talk shows, and repetitive stares.

Sometime about 1 PM on Good Friday, it occurred to me that I had to be in Florida the next Wednesday on business, and that I truly, really truly, honest to goodness, had no plan B for my father's care. It further occurred to me, that unless I found a solution to this dilemma I would have more than parent care issues to deal with when I returned.

With all the confidence that comes with ignorance, I began phoning nursing homes, geriatric centers, retirement homes (I thought they were all the same) to inquire whether there might be some room at the inn for my father. Since I had never been faced with this before, I assumed you just drove up, weekend bag in hand, with proof of insurability, a pure heart, and a small down payment, and that Dad would be greeted, treated, and checked right on in, much like a Four Seasons visit.

The next six hours were more like a visit to Dante's circle of special-care hell. Not only did I not know what questions to ask, I didn't know the language, the culture, or the raison d'être ("reason for being") of assisted-living centers. I likened it to my first trip to France, when I wanted to visit the Eiffel Tower, and the French either refused or didn't know how to speak English, and the only words I knew were *please* and *croissant*. A lawyer by training, financial advisor by occupation, and genetically wired to be an entrepreneur, I have always prided myself on my ability to outthink, outinnovate, and outperform any set of obstacles, challenges, or difficulties placed in my path. By the end of the afternoon, I had gotten some of the language, understood a little of what I needed to know and do, and made an appointment with a center in Charlotte and another in Winston-Salem. They said that if we worked diligently, we could have my dad safe and sound in his new facility by Monday.

While those visits are stories for another chapter, let me say that what was to follow after the facility decision made it seem like deciding if I wanted fries with my order.

After a restless Easter Sunday filled with a hurriedly assembled Easter basket, faux joviality, and the myopic conversation that occurs between father and son when there are no more superficial subjects to discuss, Monday and transport time arrived.

Whether my father knew he was going to a new place to live or not, I don't know and will probably never know. What I do know, and acutely remember, is that *I* knew and was completely aware that my life and my father's would never be the same.

As I walked him out to the car, I felt the emotions in the back of my throat. I helped him in, fastened his seat belt, and mumbled some excuse about having to go back in to get something. As I opened the door and shut it quickly, Christine came into the foyer and asked, "What's wrong?" The pent-up emotions of the past five days came out in a torrent of tears and gut-wrenching sobs. I cried out that I could not do this and fell on my knees in a flood of tears, rage, and frustration over what had happened. I cried for a few minutes longer, took another few moments to get myself together, and walked back out to the car to begin the two-hour ride to the Village Care facility in King, North Carolina.

During the next two hours, my father told me the same story six times, and I listened for the sixth time with the same level of attention as I had the first. It was my sixth time hearing it, but each time it was his first time telling it. I remember thinking that this must be what living in a mental institution is like. We arrived and began the in-processing that is specific to every facility of this kind in the United States. My father was not sure why he was there; all he knew was that he wanted to go home and to have me take him.

I lied that day to my father—the only lie I have ever told him. I said that he was there for a checkup and that we would go home a little bit later. By the time later got there, he had not only forgotten the lie but where he was and where home might be. As I settled him into his room, I realized I had forgotten to bring a couple of things from his home that might make him more comfortable. Things like pictures, his favorite shirt, and his table radio. While the doctors were checking him out, I asked him if there was anything else special he would like.

He said, "I want my two caps."

Surprised at the specificity of the response, I asked him which two caps out of his collection he wanted. He said that he wanted his Shriner cap. My father is a lifelong Mason in a family of Masons, and I'm sure that the cap created some security for him. I asked him what other cap he wanted me to bring. He said, "I want the Navy SEAL cap." My dad, who had been in the Navy but never a SEAL, had somehow gotten a cap with the SEAL logo on it. Curious, I asked, "Why do you want the Navy SEAL cap?"

He replied, "Because the SEALs never leave anyone behind—and I know you won't leave me behind."

This is a book about not leaving anyone behind. More importantly, it's a book about how to have the conversations, make the plans, and extend the relationship with the most important people you have ever been in a relationship with: your parents. It is a book about how to think, communicate, and take action before the inevitable time when your parents are no longer able to be responsible for themselves. It is a book about how to begin a conversation that will deepen over time.

My experience with my dad, and the mistakes I made, also showed me that I wasn't alone. This is a *big* problem. As I write these words, millions of others have already gone or are currently going through some version of my own "parent care crisis." And these instances will only increase: the parent care crisis will affect many millions more in the coming years, as we live longer and longer lives than previous generations. There needs to be a major dialog between adult children and their aging parents about how best to prepare for, and how best to be able to spend, these extra years, in terms of quality of care and quality of life. And the dialog needs to occur *now*.

The *Real* Problem

I recently read an article that admonished baby boomers for not talking to their parents about long-term care. It suggested that perhaps the subject could be brought up at dinner. I can just imagine that conversation. "Would you please pass the butter? Oh, by the way, Mom, have you chosen a nursing home yet?" The absurdity of that suggestion, however, does show why parents and children alike delay, or ignore, confronting the issue and its myriad aspects until it is often too late.

Most discussions about parent care start with decision making: i.e., what insurance policy you should buy, which nursing home you should pick, and so on. This puts the cart before the horse and leads to a plan formed in a vacuum. How are aging parents and their families to *know* which nursing home to pick—or even what to look for—without having first discussed the *why* of such a momentous decision, encompassing the many financial, emotional, and health-related issues connected with it?

Most of us, however, don't know how or where to begin this discussion because up till now there has been no model for it. The reason is that our financial and legal institutions, and the parent care industry at large, focus instead on the *support structure* (i.e., how to *write* a will) of parent care rather than on what to consider (and to anticipate) and the decision making involved in *creating* that support structure (i.e., deciding what you want the will to achieve).

This book at last puts the horse before the cart. It starts by recognizing the *real problem:* the awkwardness, the strain, the overall feeling of unease and discomfort that children and their folks have about confronting the parent care issue in the first place. It offers families a model for creating such a support structure from the ground up; one that will result in strategic rather than chaotic planning, keyed to their *specific situation* so that families can face the issue together and partake in the critical exchange necessary to ensure that the best plan is designed.

A Series of Conversations

This model consists of a series of vital conversations between children and parents on the most important long-term care topics, ranging from what to do with the parents' home and property to money and health concerns.

Focusing on the "big picture," each conversation is framed to get families to envision what they want to happen down the road as a result of the care decisions they make now, so that they make the right choices needed to get them there.

What you learn from each conversation will inform the decision-making process, enabling you and your parents to plan more effectively by doing so together *as a team,* and to feel *good* about your decisions by ensuring that the best plan is designed.

This series of conversations brings organization to what is inevitably confusing, complex, and chaotic and builds communication, clarity, collaboration, and confidence. The conversations will help you:

• Talk to your parents about their long-term care, as they age, and make plans as a family without the awkwardness and discomfort the subject usually creates

• Arrive at an accumulated agreement with resolution and consensus

• Understand all aspects of the parent care issue, from what kind of care your parents want (and you want for them) and who will provide it to often neglected legacy concerns such as how to avoid letting the issue of parent care define how you will remember your loved ones and how they wish to be remembered

• Be aware of the key timelines that will affect your decisions, the critical documents you need to prepare, the important checklists you need to make and follow, and all the other resources you need for you and your folks to design a customized parent care plan and to keep it current so that nothing is forgotten in making that plan a reality

A *Complete* Solution

The collaborative nature and conversational architecture of these discussions allow you to accomplish them in a single sitting or in a series of family meetings. Whichever way you choose, the challenges they address—on everything from quality of care to what to do with property and other assets—can be unbundled and dealt with separately so that the best possible parent care plan can be created.

By showing you how to emphasize design over default in creating your plan, you will at last have found a *complete solution* to the parent care issue, a solution flexible enough to work for anyone, in any circumstance, at any time.

A solution that ensures no family confronting the parent care crisis is left behind.

PART ONE

Opening the Door

Aging parents do not know how to discuss their economic, medical, psychological, emotional, and lifestyle requirements with their adult children, and their children are not confident about broaching any of these subjects. This is causing an expanding number of family-stressful maladies including neglect, estrangement, bankruptcy, poverty, guilt, resentment, and depression.

—Dan Sullivan, The Strategic Coach, Inc.

1

Excuses, Excuses

Procrastination is the art of keeping up with yesterday.

—Don Marquis, humorist

Situation Normal, All Fouled Up

Tim Johnson's mom and dad were typical Depression-era parents. Tim's dad was a manager at a local pipe-fitting plant for nearly forty years. Having started out as a laborer, through his own drive and initiative he eventually become plant manager of the family-owned concern. Tim's dad retired nearly seven years ago, with a comfortable pension and the promise of a comfortable, if not extravagant, retirement.

Tim's mom retired a year before Tim's dad, after a thirty-five-year career as a registered nurse at a local hospital. Together, they are able to cover all their bills and even have some money left over for trips, gifts for the grandkids, and their church tithe. Nevertheless, like many who grew up in the Great Depression, they have never felt economically secure. As a result, money has always been a taboo subject within the family.

Over the past several years, Tim approached his parents obliquely on numerous occasions about whether they had their affairs in order and whether there was anything they needed to do to make sure that things continued to go as they wanted them to in the future. Tim's dad reassured him each time that the family lawyer had "taken care of everything," and that all the documents needed were "locked down tight" in a safe place. When Tim pressed his father for copies of those documents, however, his dad would always reply, "They're in storage. I'll get 'em for you next week." But "next week" would never come.

Tim was unable to press his mom about this because she left the family finances and legal affairs up to her husband. In fact, the only checks she'd written since getting married were for the groceries and the electricity bill. Though concerned about whether his dad really did have everything in order, Tim didn't want to confront him and potentially create a scene. Instead, he chose to trust that his dad knew what he was doing. Then the unexpected happened.

Tim's mom and dad were involved in a car accident on their way to church. Tim's dad was severely injured and lapsed into a coma from which he has not yet emerged. The doctors are not sure if he will come out of it but consider it likely that if he does, he will be paralyzed from the waist down due to his injuries. Tim's mom suffered a head injury that has limited her speech, voice, and cognitive abilities. She remains in critical care in the intensive care unit of the same hospital where she worked for thirty-five years.

Upon hearing of the accident from a neighbor, Tim immediately called the hospital only to be told that unless he had a health care power of attorney on behalf of his father and mother, no one would be able to speak with him directly.

Tim frantically began searching his parents' home for the documents his dad had told him were all in order. He finally found a box marked "important papers." Inside were his parents' respective wills and a living will, a general power of attorney, and a health care power of attorney—everything his dad had assured him was "locked down tight." Except that they weren't as "locked down" as his dad thought: *none of the documents was signed!*

There was a four-year-old letter from the family lawyer instructing Tim's parents to sign the documents, but no follow-up correspondence. When Tim called the lawyer's office, he was told the man had retired and that his records, if there were any, had been placed in storage.

Thinking the local bank might be able to help, Tim went there, but the branch manager, while sympathetic to Tim's plight, was prohibited by bank policy from discussing a client's affairs with anyone without *signed* authorization.

Tim's next course of action was to seek out an elder care law attorney who specialized in such matters to see if he could break the impasse. After thumbing through the phone book, he finally located one, who, for a retainer of $5,000, said he would begin proceedings with the court to have Tim appointed as guardian. The lawyer told Tim that it could take as long as ten days to get before a judge, even for an emergency hearing, and cautioned him that even though Tim was the Johnsons' son, when they did get a hearing it would not be an automatic decision on the part of the court to appoint him guardian. Tim had no choice but to adopt a wait-and-see attitude.

In the interim, the hospital was treating his parents under what is called a "prudent professional" standard of care, meaning the hospital's lawyers have advised the doctors not to do anything that "could come back to haunt the hospital later." Tim could continue to visit his parents, of course, but until the court order was issued declaring him guardian, he was not able to obtain any essential information from the attending nurses, aides, or staff physician. He could only look on helplessly as his father and mother received this "do no harm" standard of care.

While this story may seem extreme, even almost contrived, every word of it is true. Worse still, cases like it occur throughout the United States, Canada, and most of the industrialized world every day. The moral of the story is that parents who think they are shielding their children from worry and stress by not discussing the realities of their situation with them are only setting their children up for worry and stress when the you-know-what hits the fan. And the children they want to shield only compound the problem for themselves and their parents by going along, or making possibly false assumptions, so as not to rock the boat.

The Nine Common Excuses for Doing Nothing

In this chapter I'll share with you the nine most common excuses people just like Tim and his parents make for avoiding or not following through on the parent care issue. Often, people are not even aware of making these excuses. Being aware of them, however, is the first step toward getting beyond them and opening the door for a frank and useful conversation.

See if any of these excuses resonate by reminding you of your family situation.

EXCUSE 1: *"My parents have money, property, and papers scattered all over the place. Even they aren't sure where everything is. There's no way to deal with a situation like that."*

This is called the "all must be perfect" syndrome. Unless your parents are accountants or engineers, the odds of finding their important records stored away neatly in boxes for you, arranged chronologically and fully indexed according to subject matter, are pretty slim. Most parents are like Tim's—and worse. Their record-keeping methods resemble the chaos of the fall of Saigon. The creation, in recent years, of software tools for improving money-management strategies and keeping better financial records has only ensured one thing: your hunt now will be for digital *as well as* hard copies of important family documents. I'll give you an example.

Ken and Beth Spratt have kept their financial affairs separate throughout most of their married life. Ken has his own checking account, Beth has hers, but they now have a joint account they use for common household bills. Over the years, they have both kept pretty good records but in different ways. Ken has his on the computer (he changes his password each month), with hard copies kept in a mini-storage unit to which he has the only key. Beth takes care of her checkbook as well as the joint checking account records, but over time she grew weary of the filing and started putting these records in boxes with the aim of "getting to them" some rainy day.

Ken and Beth executed wills, powers of attorney, and living wills ten years ago; they keep them at a local bank in a safety deposit box to which they have a key that, they maintain, they can put their hands on in a moment's notice. And even if the key went missing, Ben has a friend at the bank he *just knows* would give their children access to the box if necessary.

The excuse that's really at work here is called "life." The manner in which many people go about organizing and updating their financial affairs and records often resembles that familiar vacation spot called Someday Isle. The net result for the child, who must parachute in and find everything when an emergency arises, or organize assets for distribution following the death of a parent, can sometimes be like a scavenger hunt. In order to find the last house payment made, it may become necessary to sift through months of statements covering a host of expenses, ranging from gas bills and car payments to American Legion dues and Colonial Penn's guaranteed issue term life premiums. And typically, this must all be accomplished at a moment of maximum personal stress. So, what is a child to do if he or she has parents like Ken and Beth?

The worst thing to do is to follow in their footsteps and do nothing. The emotional toll and financial consequences can be disastrous (for more on this, see chapters 5 and 8, The Property Conversation" and "The Legacy Conversation"). Here are some general tips for getting your folks off the dime with regard to organizing their important papers and making sure they are easy to locate:

• If you are skilled at organizing and it comes easy to you, offer to put your folks' papers in order as a present, instead of giving your mom that third set of designer dish towels or your dad that cardigan sweater he won't wear. It's a present that will help not only them but you too.

• On the other hand, if, like your parents (and most humans), you get a Dubious Achievement Award for organizing, then hire a professional organizer to do it for your folks and make that your gift. In fact, maybe you can get a package deal for yourself. It will pay off in the end. See chapter 5, "The Property Conversation," for help finding one in your area.

• Put your own affairs in order, and tell your parents how good doing this made you feel about finally knowing everything's been taken care of and where it is—hint, hint.

• Explain to your folks that by not keeping their affairs up-to-date and easily accessible so that you can help them when the time comes, they are creating a potentially dangerous situation where no one will be able to help anybody.

• If all else fails, pull out the stops. Tell them that without access to their records, particularly their checkbook, you might not even be able to bury them; you might have to put them in storage instead! They'll think you're kidding . . . at first.

EXCUSE 2: *"My parents say they've already worked things out with their attorney and don't need to do it again."*

This excuse is a variation on the one you made about bathing or brushing your teeth when you were five years old: you did it once really well, so there's no need to do it again. Here's a real-world example of the consequences of this type of thinking.

For thirty years, Pat and Sandy Caseman have used the same attorney for everything, from having their wills drawn up when they were first married to handling the real estate closings on their various residences and vacation homes. The problem is that they haven't reviewed and updated their estate planning and property ownership documents since. What would occur if either Pat or Sandy were to die or become incapacitated? Some assets are owned by Pat, some by Sandy; some properties are owned jointly and some in partnership with other couples. Titles to their automobiles are held by various corporate entities and ownership of some of those entities has changed, a common occurrence that is not reflected in their estate documents. Why? Because they just tell their lawyer, "Make sure this goes in our file, OK?" It may go in, or it may not. Either way, it's not enough.

What's behind this scenario is an assumption many of us make: that once something has been done, it may never again have to be revisited and redone—or if it does, that there is plenty of time to do so. We also assume it's the attorney's job, not ours, to stay on top of our affairs and that he or she will "take care of things automatically." But the most dangerous assumption we make is that the attorney will handle everything we expect of him or her *correctly.*

My experience with estate attorneys particularly, is that they are long on explanation, adequate with execution, and almost nonexistent when it comes to follow-up that is not initiated by the client. Most will notify clients of major changes to tax law (typically via the firm's newsletter or an e-mail or fax communication), but often that's as far as it goes. It is usually left to the client to set the wheels in motion for taking action and scheduling an appointment.

Estate attorneys are notorious for not doing work automatically; they do not want to rock the boat by sending unexpected bills to clients, who often balk at receiving such bills no matter how much they want their attorneys to "take care of things automatically." As a result, many elder clients, though alerted to the need to update their affairs, may go years without seeing their attorney and wind up doing nothing. With some documents this may not matter. But with critical legal and estate documents such as general powers of attorney, health care directives, living wills, and so on, if the documents are not continually reviewed and updated to reflect the parents' current state of affairs, the impact on the family may be catastrophic.

What can you do to get beyond this excuse? Ask to see a copy of the most recent estate documents your parents have executed. This will tell you how recent those documents really are. Even though you may not be a lawyer, you can check for the following:

1. Are all the documents signed, dated, and, if necessary, notarized?
2. Are you named in the documents in any way (such as executor) that will require you to understand what your rights and responsibilities are?
3. Do you share powers and responsibilities with other siblings or parties?

Since it is ultimately you who will be accountable, it is you who should assume immediate responsibility for verifying the existence and accuracy of the legal and estate documents your parents purport to have completed. If your folks drag their feet in producing them, say you will resign all the responsibilities you've been given in those documents should something happen. That is usually enough to make the documents appear for your examination.

EXCUSE 3: *"My parents are very private about their financial situation. It was a taboo subject when I was growing up. I can't get them to open up now."*

Oakley and Margaret Hartland have retired comfortably but far from luxuriously, having raised three children on a railroad worker's salary and a substitute teacher's stipend. They often went without or had to borrow money from friends to make ends meet. None of their children had any idea of the sacrifices their parents made to give them a good life, and that's the way their folks wanted it. Now, as the couple is getting older and seeing what little savings they managed to put aside dwindling, they are *embarrassed* to share the true state of their financial affairs with their children, whose help they will indeed need not very far down the road. They are afraid their kids will think badly of them.

Here's what's going on. All parents want their kids to think they have done well in life financially. No parents that I know want to lay the burden of their fiscal problems on their kids. If the news is bad, they want to shield this information from their kids. Even if the news is good, they typically don't talk about it. Part of this is due to the irony that even though we in America are consumed by the almighty buck, we are extremely reluctant to discuss our financial situation at any length or in any detail with those closest to us. We don't want them to know how much or how little of the almighty buck we have. People will gab on and on about their vacations, their children, their ailments, job insecurities, and religious beliefs, to family and even strangers, but will not, it seems, except under penalty of death, reveal having $2,700 in a savings account somewhere.

In this book, I penetrate that wall by treating money (see chapter 4, "The Money Conversation") strictly as a tool. I don't make judgments about whether the tool your parents have is good, bad, big, or little. I focus instead on using what there is to build on. Thus, the conversation shifts away from money as a taboo subject, indicative of power, prestige, and status (or lack thereof), to thinking of money as something like a screwdriver, a chisel, a saw, or some other building tool.

EXCUSE 4: *"My parents and I have never been close, have never been able to talk about anything, and rarely see each other. It's too late to start a relationship now."*

Taylor Johnson and his wife Elizabeth have had very successful careers as executives working in Fortune 500 companies. He retired as president of a large industrial glass-making concern and she as a successful director of human resources for an international consulting firm. They have lived and traveled first class most of their lives, occasionally spending time abroad with their children, who attended various boarding and prep schools. A nanny or other member of the Johnson household staff typically looked after the children when they were growing up. As a result, the children have a cordial but not exactly intimate relationship with their parents. They respect their folks, admire them, even love them, but don't really connect with them. And now that their folks are aging, the children are reluctant and insecure about engaging them in an intimate conversation about the challenges ahead. As much as the children would like to raise the care issue, they really don't know how—in a way, it seems more normal to hand off the responsibility to their parents' staff, just as the staff took care of their needs when they were growing up.

It has been my experience that children at either end of the economic spectrum, rich or poor, wish to have had a "better past" as far as their relationship with their parents is concerned. But the cold, hard fact is: the past is past; there is no going back. It's the present that counts.

As long as you and your parents are breathing, there is an opportunity to communicate and build, not a "better past," but a "better future" with each other—or at the very least to improve upon your relationship. Maybe the damage is done and communication is no longer possible. You won't know until you try. Chapter 7 ("The Professional Care Conversation") will show you how to reduce your feelings of insecurity and reluctance about broaching the care issue with your parents if you feel estranged from them. It gives you a structure for opening the door to having a genuine discussion based not on past experience but on future expectations.

EXCUSE 5: *"I don't have any siblings and can't do this by myself."*
Ashley Townsend is a thirty-five-year-old only child, born when her mother was forty and her father forty-five. Her par-

ents had successful careers, as a college professor and dentist, respectively, and decided they wanted a child to round out their life experience.

Ashley was thus showered with attention, material goods, and the kind of protection typical of children with affluent parents. As a result, she is well-educated, well-mannered, financially self-sufficient, and, for the most part, incapable of grasping the idea that there is anyone else on this planet but her. In fact, one of her fundamental beliefs is that when she closes her eyes, it is the world that can't see her. The concept of being the caregiver to her parents is as foreign to her now as the thought of driving a used car was in high school.

Being an only child is a mixed blessing. Growing up, you receive all the attention, money, and opportunity without having to share them with any pesky siblings. But during the last part of your parents' lives, you have all the obligations, responsibilities, and duties of caring for them, without any siblings to help pick up the slack.

Instead of making an excuse about why you can't do this by yourself, turn it into a question: "If *I* don't do this for my parents, who will?" This opens the door to considering options. You never know, there may even be a person you hadn't thought of, outside the family, who could lend you a helping hand once in a while or at least provide moral support.

Recognize this: at some point in your parents' situation, *decisions will have to be made.* If not, messes will have to be cleaned up due to the decisions that weren't made. Get over the idea that the parent care situation would be easier to deal with and free of internal and external conflict "if only there was someone else." It's not that kind of situation and not that kind of planet.

EXCUSE 6: *"My family is very close-knit. Everyone will want to be involved or, at a minimum, informed about what's going on. You know what they say about 'too many cooks': things will just get out of control."*

Juan and Anita Alvarez are retired guidance counselors in their seventies, living in a small Southern California town. The Alvarezes have six children (three girls, three boys), all married with children, successful, and as close as siblings can be; they vacation together.

Juan and Anita are beginning to show their age, however, and are experiencing some of the symptoms of people who have worked hard all their lives to raise a family, often neglecting their own health in the process. For example, Juan is beginning to exhibit signs of dementia, and Anita has had two hip-replacement surgeries within the last several years. The children have hired a housekeeper and a yardman to help their folks out, but they worry that this may not be enough, that it's just not safe anymore for their parents to live alone, even with help. But the prospect of so many voices involved in making decisions about their care (all six siblings, their spouses, plus Juan and Anita) makes the entire family jumpy about potential conflict that could drive them apart.

The fact is this: the Alvarez family probably has a greater chance of jointly creating and managing a parent care solution without undue conflict and harm to their relationships than do many smaller families with fewer siblings. This is because the Alvarezes have everything working for them: (1) they are a close-knit family; (2) there is ongoing, positive interaction among and between siblings and spouses; and (3) as evidenced by their jointly hiring a housekeeper and yardman for their parents, they already show a harmonious, collaborative commitment to their parents' well-being.

The challenge for them is to come up with a decision-making structure in which everyone has a vote, but no one can create gridlock. For example, they could establish a family management trust, in which three of the siblings form the executive committee and all six are board members. That way, everyone gets to voice an opinion and vote, but in the end it is up to the three members of the executive committee to make the final decisions based on a minimum two to one majority (for more on this, see chapter 7, "The Professional Care Conversation").

Think positively. If yours is a family with lots of siblings, focus not on how many voices there are to create potential conflict and chaos but on how wonderful it is that there are *so many* of you who can and want to help!

EXCUSE 7: *"I have my own life and my own responsibilities to take care of, and just can't do this."*

Elizabeth Chadwick is a forty-two-year-old mother of three, ages twelve, nine, and seven. Her husband, Arthur, is national sales manager for a large pharmaceutical firm and travels four days out of five during the week. On at least three weekends a month, the Chadwicks entertain physicians who prescribe, and who are the major distributors of, the firm's products. Between helping with homework, soccer practice, dance lessons, T-ball, and entertaining clients, Elizabeth is sure that least 120 percent of her time is accounted for.

Adding to this, her parents are exhibiting signs of failing health and dementia, and are rapidly approaching the point where they will no longer be able to manage for themselves on a day-to-day basis. Currently, a home health care agency is providing minor assistance, but her parents depend on Elizabeth psychologically and physically for emotional support and transportation. As a result, there are moments when Elizabeth feels like she is at the absolute end of her rope.

Well, her rope is only going to get a lot shorter and her life more intense as her parents make the complete transition from living independently with some assistance to being totally dependent in an assisted-living situation. Welcome, Elizabeth, to the brave new world where many of us will spend as long a time taking care of our parents as they did raising us.

The two care situations, however, are 180 degrees apart. As children, we move gradually from dependence to interdependence to independence. But as parents, we move from independence to interdependence to complete dependence on our children.

Elizabeth has only begun to experience the dynamics of this shift. Up to now, she has just been a member of the audience in that play called "Her Parents' Life." Rapidly, she is now moving toward becoming a full-blown member of the cast. She is about to come face-to-face with a dramatic change in the demand on her time and energy and on her perspective as she moves from an increasingly less passive role in her parents' care to an increasingly more active one.

Her default position could be to excuse herself as being way too busy, way too tired, or way too involved with other responsibilities to be able to handle this too. To that excuse, my response is: Who doesn't feel overloaded from time to time? This isn't about *you! It's about your parents!* How about stepping up to the plate and taking a leadership role in bringing a sense of confidence to the situation? How about being the person your parents invested *their* time, *their* energy, *their* money, and *their* love raising you to become? How about using the situation not as an opportunity to indulge in self-pity but for growing and developing additional reserves of character, strength, and integrity?

EXCUSE 8: *"I can't deal with the hurt and pain of talking to my parents about the end of their lives."*

Seeing the parent care situation as the end of the line for your parents is making a judgment that life is simply over for us as we deeply age. *Life isn't over. It is just different.* A centenarian has a future, even if it's just measured in mealtimes. As that baseball-playing philosopher Yogi Berra tells us, "It ain't over 'til it's over."

We tend to think that because our aging folks can no longer hop to the convenience store, mow the lawn, or sing in the choir, life for them has simply become one long, passive wait at the station for that next train to forever. But how about focusing instead on what is possible, not what's impossible. OK, so your seventy-year-old dad no longer has the pipes to sing in the choir. He can still talk, can't he? He can still communicate and interact with you and other people. No, it may not be possible any longer for him to satisfy his appetite for faraway places by traveling to them. But he can still read about them, still be an armchair explorer via the Travel and National Geographic channels. He can still learn and talk about the places that interest him even if he can't physically go there. Similarly, while it may no longer be possible for your seventy-year-old mom to attend to her garden outside, she can still tend to her flowers indoors. As long as you consider the idea of a tomorrow, you can plan to make the most of the reality of it.

Robert Aldridge, for example, has watched his aging father's life go from including a broad range of activities and a large circle of friends to a narrower range of activities and a smaller circle of friends. Part of this change is due to his father's worsening emphysema and the natural attrition that occurs among any aging group of acquaintances. Rather than accept these changes as signposts of his dad's end, however, Robert has seized the opportunity to help his father (and thus himself) through the transition. He both encourages and has even participated in getting his father to create a community of new friends and acquaintances within the assisted-living center where his father now lives.

Once an avid gardener and feeder of the neighborhood squirrels, his father has now taken to tending a miniature greenhouse (supplied by his son) in his room. Through this activity he has become quite popular as the so-called gardener in residence at the center, where he goes from room to room with his watering cart and pruning tools, helping others attend to their plants, finding opportunities in the process to make friends and expand his interests. Instead of feeding the squirrels, he now watches them from the center's solarium or through binoculars from his room. Is everything the same as before for the elderly man? No. Is it better? Who knows? Is it different and interesting? Most assuredly it is; different from and more interesting than just doing nothing but waiting for that next train to forever to arrive.

If you think a scenario like this is not possible for *your* parents and thereby excuse yourself, you will be right. The key to overcoming this and every other excuse for inaction on the parent care issue is not to focus on what we think is true but on what can be *made* to become true.

EXCUSE 9: *"I have never been good with money. I wouldn't want to be responsible for any advice or decision making in that area on my parents' behalf."*

Andrea and John Simpson have been married for twenty-five years and have two children in college. The Simpsons enjoy life to the fullest, using their money to travel, keep a nice home, and provide for their children. As a result, they live pretty much paycheck to paycheck, never going too deeply into debt but never saving too much either, except for contributions to their respective company retirement plans. Neither of them feels especially adept at, or even comfortable, managing their own money, let alone someone else's.

Recently, Andrea's dad was diagnosed with late-stage dementia and early-stage Alzheimer's. He has asked her to take over the day-to-day paying of bills and management of his assets (almost $400,000) because he feels he is becoming less and less confident in his own ability to do those things. Andrea is panic-stricken at the prospect of this. She is fearful of screwing up and making a costly mistake that will bring the wrath of her younger brother and half-sister down on her in the form of a lawsuit after her dad is gone.

Here's the straight dope. There is no reason for Andrea to take a pass because she feels uneasy about her lack of money-management skills. In fact, the realization that she isn't good at handling money is an important first step to competently handling her dad's affairs as he wishes. She just has to take the next step; i.e., to find someone who has those skills and to hire that person to help her. There are almost limitless options out there in the form of do-it-yourself software and other resources and safeguards to aid money-management-challenged people today. Many members of the financial planning and insurance industries and the legal and accounting professions are fast developing capabilities in this area just so they can provide such services to people like Andrea (see chapter 4, "The Money Conversation").

No More Excuses

Excuses are justifications for not taking control of a situation, for opting to do nothing instead of something so as to avoid assuming responsibility and accountability. In this case, however, since the subject is parent care, no matter how many excuses you make, responsibility and accountability will one day be thrust upon you anyway. You might as well act now.

To keep on making excuses is simply to prepare the way for suddenly finding yourself in the middle of a situation you *must* handle *now,* and for which, through your avoidance, you are totally unprepared.

So, as the Boy Scouts' motto says: "Be prepared." It's in your own best interest, not to mention the right thing to do, to stop playing head games with yourself and making excuses for inaction—and to start taking control of your parents' protection as they age, just as they did for you when you were growing up.

2

The CARE "Hear and Now"
Listening System

*Learning is a result of listening, which in turn leads to even
better listening and attentiveness to the other person.*

—Alice Miller, psychoanalyst

Can You Hear Me Now?

William Salvone is a successful seventy-year-old businessman,
now retired from the machine-manufacturing industry. A self-
made man, he is someone who, in his own words, "has no time
for idiots or people who know them." He attributes his success
to an ability to see a solution, get what's needed to put that solution in place, and then move on to the next project. He is
long on intelligence, short on patience, and all his life has practiced a communication style that falls somewhere between that
of a NATO commander and a junior high school principal—a
style his son, Robert, grew up experiencing on a daily basis. As
a result, Robert early on developed a habit of pretending to listen to his dad's one-way conversations while in reality his attention was a million miles away. All he had to do to convince his
dad that he was hanging on the man's every word was slap a

smile on his face and now and then interject a "really," a "tell me more," an "I didn't know that," or a "you're kidding." It is a practice that Robert has carried with him even into adulthood.

The problem now is that even as father and son experience the fact of the father's aging, the same old patterns of communication continue. And the father has now caught on to the fact that often his son is only half-listening to him. The same goes for other members of the family, who only half-listen to him as well. At a time of life when communication with others is so critical, he anguishes over being tuned out so much of the time (even if he did bring it on himself), seeing this as an acknowledgment by the people around him that he has nothing important to say. And so he clams up. William and his son now find themselves, as the Dave Mason song goes, "sitting here together, miles apart as time goes slipping by."

Either as parents or as children, all of us can identify with this story in some way. That's because as kids we grow up being told what to do by our folks. Certainly by our teenage years, we respond to this much of the time by turning a deaf (or semi-deaf) ear to what they say to us. Then we repeat this process with our own kids, only now we're the ones doing the telling, and they're the ones doing the half-listening.

Hearing someone without actually listening to them isn't practiced only by parents and their kids, however. Siblings and friends, husbands and wives, employers and employees engage in it too. We're *all* guilty of it at some time or another. In fact, today, hearing but not listening is almost the norm, exacerbated by the cacophony of visual and auditory "noise" that surrounds us, competing for our attention and consuming every centimeter of available space and every decibel of available bandwidth.

Between aging parents and their grown children especially, there is a crying need for a system capable of breaking down this communication roadblock—a way for them to be able to open the door and converse with one another about important issues such as parent care in a way that actively promotes responsive listening.

Now there is.

"Hear and Now" Listening with CARE

Think about the listening experience this way: Remember the last time you saw a really good movie—you know, the kind that grabs you from the opening credits, pulling you into its world and its characters, making you part of the experience? Imagine how different that experience would be if a different movie with a different story and different characters were suddenly superimposed over it. That is what happens when you half-listen.

When people converse with you, they are inviting you in to see and experience the movie going on inside their heads. By not being fully present and engaged—an active listener—you miss important chunks and significant details of that movie because you are superimposing your own movie over theirs. Do this often enough, particularly with older people, and they will simply shut down, like William did in the previous story. You need to create an environment where this won't happen, an environment that encourages your parents to open up to you about their concerns and fears about the future (where previously they might not otherwise have been inclined to do so), and for you to really *hear* them, without missing a beat.

The system I have developed to achieve this grew out of the experience I had with my own dad's care, which I explained in the introduction to this book. It is a system structured around the acronym CARE, which stands for the following: challenges, alternatives, resources, and experience. (CARE makes them easy to remember.) This system will help you elicit telling responses from your parents on key issues relating to their future care—even those about which they may not have been forthcoming up to now—so that you get what you need to be able to work together to achieve a mutually satisfying parent care solution.

Let's look at the individual components of the CARE "hear and now" listening system:

• **Challenges.** It is typical of older people to point out dozens of reasons why something won't or can't work rather than how to make it work. That's why the CARE system begins here. It recognizes the fact that as we grow older we tend to see change of almost any sort—but especially changes in ourselves physically, mentally, or in our lifestyle—as an insurmountable obstacle, a series of doors slamming shut rather than opening. We don't even want to think about these changes, much less talk about them. The objective here is to refocus your parents' thinking about their future in terms of what they *want* to happen when that future comes and not just what they fear will go awry. The idea is, if you can get them to articulate their feelings and fears about the future and to anticipate inevitable changes as a series of challenges rather than insurmountable obstacles to be dreaded, then maybe they will begin to find ways of meeting those challenges and achieving what they want for their future instead of feeling that defeat is inevitable.

• **Alternatives.** There *are* options available to meet the challenges your parents face. By getting your parents to focus on what they *can* do rather than on all the reasons why they can't do something, you will help them to feed off the positive energy they gain from this, and their minds will naturally kick into idea-sorting/problem-solving mode. The more alternatives to each challenge they consider, the more confidence they will develop that they can successfully take on these challenges, giving them the self-assurance to move forward.

• **Resources.** I love the movie *Castaway* starring Tom Hanks. In it, he plays a FedEx employee who crash-lands in the ocean and suddenly finds himself stranded on an island with almost nothing to rely on for survival but his wits. He learns to fish and make shelter, to withstand severe rainstorms and extreme sun, and even fashions a companion to talk to from a soccer ball that made it to shore with him. The resources component of CARE does much the same thing; it enables your parents see that, like Tom Hanks in the movie, they are in possession of and have access to more resources than they ever imagined (of their own and from elsewhere) for addressing the challenges they face.

• **Experience.** Based on the challenges they have anticipated, the alternatives they know they have, and the resources they now know are available to them, the last step in the CARE process is for your parents to lay out a series of realistic outcomes they can reasonably expect if they start taking action now. In other words, here is where you get your parents to visualize the *experience* they want to have as the result of meeting each challenge head-on. Armed with this knowledge, you can plan together as a family to bring that experience to fruition.

The Parent Care Conversations

The CARE "hear and now" listening system is all about asking the *right* questions now in order to avoid confusion and conflict later on from chaotic decision making. In part 2, you will learn

❖ The Odds of Miscommunicating

The potential for miscommunication between people is staggering, especially when we consider that of the estimated 800,000 words in the English language, we use only about eight hundred of them consistently. And there are, on average, between fifteen and seventeen meanings in the dictionary, and in our vernacular, for each of those words. This means that even conservatively speaking, we have a one in seventeen chance of being misunderstood. Further complicating matters, approximately 55 percent of what we communicate is transmitted nonverbally, via gestures, facial expressions, a lifted eyebrow, a look in the eyes; 38 percent is communicated by the tone, rhythm, and pacing of how we speak; and only 7 percent is communicated through words. This is why being fully present and engaged ("hear and now" listening) is central to getting your parents to open up to you (and thereby to themselves) on the issue of future care—and for you to *really* take in what they are telling you—so that strategic planning becomes possible.

how to apply this system in framing your questions for the six key conversations you must have with your parents in order to work toward an effective solution. These six parent care conversations are structured around the six fundamental areas parents need to be concerned about in contemplating their future care—and that you need information on in order to empower your parents to play a meaningful role in the design of their own long-term care solution, and not just be bystanders.

The six conversations and their objectives are:

1. The Big Picture Conversation. It all starts with your parents having a vision of their future and your knowing what that vision is. If your parents have shared very little or nothing with you about how they see their future and the issue of their future care, then there isn't much to discuss, is there? This conversation is all about getting that discussion going, about getting your parents to reveal how they see the rest of their lives unfolding so that their fears and concerns, hopes and dreams are broadly exposed for all of you to address.

2. The Money Conversation. This is a biggie. The objective here is to obtain an overall grasp of your parents' current financial situation, their future financial needs, and the financial structure they will need to create in order to maximize the growth and income opportunities of their financial resources.

3. The Property Conversation. This discussion focuses on looking at (and perhaps inventorying) what your parents have collected over the years in terms of property and possessions, and determining how they would like that property to be managed and/or distributed, both in the years they have left and after they're gone.

4. The House Conversation. This can be an extremely emotional issue. The objective is to get a fix on how your parents feel about their ability to keep living where they are now. For example, is their home already, or do they see it becoming, a physical or financial burden? If so, what is their preferred next step? Staying but with help or selling and moving? And if the latter, to where: a newer, smaller home, a retirement community, an assisted-living facility, or perhaps a special care facility?

5. The Professional Care Conversation. This discussion follows directly on the house conversation if the decision to move to an assisted-living facility, nursing home, or other institutional setting is immediate or in the cards. It focuses on the type of care your parents will need (thus determining the setting) and the type of attention (visitation and other considerations) your parents would like (and can reasonably expect) from you depending upon where they relocate, so that your relationship does not become strained and distant but even closer.

6. The Legacy Conversation. This last conversation gets your parents thinking about their lives, their achievements, the journey they have made through life so far, and considering how they want to be remembered by family, friends, and the organizations to which they either belonged or donated. The legacy conversation is where they start laying the groundwork for creating and preserving that legacy through declaration of assets, making gifts and other bequests, and numerous other methods.

By confronting the daunting, seemingly unmanageable issue of long-term care planning in this unique conversational style, you and your parents will be able to:

- Cut the issue down to size, transforming fear into focused thinking and strategic planning
- Perceive what you initially thought were weaknesses in the situation as strengths instead
- Turn potential obstacles into opportunities for innovation
- Fashion breakthroughs out of setbacks that may occur along the way
- Deal with every challenge, consider every alternative, and maximize every resource at hand to design the long-term care experience your parents *want* to have!

In short, in place of silence and dread, chaos and confusion over the parent care issue, you and your folks will be able to substitute absolute, unremitting, and total confidence in your ability to handle that issue successfully.

Initiating the Parent Care Conversations

Talking to the elderly about aging is a lot like talking to the poor about poverty; no matter how delicately we approach the subject, we run the risk of scaring, offending, or outright alienating them merely by bringing it up. Therefore, initiating the parent care conversations is not simply a matter of choosing a time and place (though each are important), then launching in, but of careful preparation. Here are some suggestions for how to prepare:

• **Work on *your* mind-set first.** At all costs, you want to avoid coming across in an intrusive or invasive manner. This manner only communicates the following message, one that is a real turn-off: "Listen, Mom and Dad, I have thought everything through about your future care on your behalf, have come up with all the answers, and only need you to affirm my conclusions." This approach is guaranteed to alienate anybody; take it up with your parents and they are sure to put you off for more urgent subjects of interest like weeding the backyard or wetlands planning. Put yourself in their shoes. The whole idea is to partner with your parents, to help them strategize about their own future care. It is not to be a vendor or pitchman for a particular product or approach. That's what the legal and financial services industries are all about. The structure of each parent care conversation is designed to help you become that partner, but before engaging your parents in discussion, you must first open yourself to seeing all the facets of that discussion from *their* perspective, not yours, so that the plans you collectively make will be a reflection of their thoughts, their ideas, their feelings, and their goals, not some boilerplate solution that says, "Here's what you need to do to be OK."

• **Easy does it.** The parent care conversations are designed to open you and your parents up to achieving deeper and deeper levels of intimacy in order to arrive at a clear, mutual understanding of your respective feelings about the issue of future care. To penetrate these levels, it is best to ease in at first by talking to your parents in abstract terms about elder care—as if the time to get down to brass tacks and actually start making plans to confront the issue were yet years away, not here knocking at the door. This approach is less intimidating for all concerned and really helps open up communication. The big-picture conversation facilitates this because it not only takes the abstract approach, but it does so in the broadest terms, which is why it is the first conversation in line.

• **Pick a time and place that best suits the conversation.** The kitchen or dining room table, at night or on a weekend, is a great place to have the money conversation. It's an informal setting used for family gatherings, and there's plenty of room to spread out financial records and other papers so everyone can see and discuss them. Or, you might select the patio or porch on a lazy afternoon as the perfect place (and time) to have the legacy conversation. Choose whatever works to create the most relaxed, reflective atmosphere possible.

The Heart of the Matter

The Wilson family of Fayetteville, North Carolina, is a good example of how the CARE system, when applied to these six conversations, really gets to the heart of the matter—the deep-down concerns parents have as they age and the impact their aging has on their children as the family moves through this life transition together.

Leonard Wilson has been a tobacco farmer all his life. He comes from a family of tobacco farmers going all the way back to before North Carolina became a state. Now seventy-four, Leonard's memory isn't what it used to be. It takes him a little longer to get going in the morning on the walks he takes with his wife, Betty, also in her seventies. He is at a place where there are many unspoken things he has long wanted to say to his family—about the future of the farm and his relationships with his children—that he fears it may be too late to say, even if he knew how. Tension has developed between him and his oldest son, Ben, over the old man having sold off parcels of acreage to developers over the years at less than maximum value rather than holding out for a higher price, which Ben had always urged. But as his father told him: "Holding out for a while as you get older feels a lot scarier than holding out for a while at forty-five. A bird in the hand is important."

The root of the tension between Ben and his father lies not so much in their ongoing differences of opinion on financial matters, however, but in the fact that the two of them are so much alike. Both are strong-willed and full of opinions (all of them right), possessed of all the answers (mostly to questions never asked), and free with their advice (to which neither of them listens). In short, they can't communicate.

Even though his father was skeptical when Ben approached him about the CARE system and the six parent care conversations, the old man agreed to listen, and then to participate. The result, he and his son would later say, was a transforming experience for each of them, and for the entire family as well.

During the conversations with Ben and his other children (Allison and Charles), Leonard talked about the small fortune he had amassed over the years by shopping frugally and saving well. Not only had every mortgage he'd ever taken out on the farm been paid off years ago, but unbeknownst to his children, he had their college funds completely established by the time they graduated high school. Thus, the reasons why his father had sold off acreage at lower prices for ready cash at last became clear to Ben.

The children were amused to find out that their father had pretended to be broke and made them take out college loans— only to pay off those loans himself when they graduated— because he wanted to make sure they were as committed to finishing their education as he was to providing for it.

Further, Leonard and his wife revealed how long they saw themselves staying at the farm until it became unsafe for them to do so. That day, they admitted, was coming soon, and when it came, they would like to go to the Shriner's Village, an assisted-living facility nearby. This way they would still be close by for family visits and holidays while at the same time being in a secure facility geared to the needs and challenges of older folks like them.

On the subject of family visits, they revealed how often they would like their kids to come and visit—at least once a month—and that they would use e-mail to communicate with their children and grandchildren on a regular basis.

They talked about what to do with all the "stuff" they had accumulated over the years, not just the things they wanted distributed after they were gone, like clothes and shoes, and years of accumulated *National Geographic* magazines (Leonard's so-called rainy day books), but things they wanted to give away while they were still living. Leonard's two Labrador dogs, for example. They didn't do much but sleep and eat, but he loved them anyway, and he wanted to be sure that when he and his wife got to the point where they couldn't take care of the dogs anymore, whoever took the dogs would keep the pair together. Ben—with whom Leonard had always had the most communication problems—said he completely understood his dad's attitude and in a surprise gesture added that he would take the two dogs himself, since he and his wife had been looking at dogs for some time.

The family then began designing a plan for inventorying everything so that the children would know what their parents wanted to stay in the family and what they wanted given away. In this way, there would be no gray areas that might lead to upset feelings later on, and everybody got the chance to put in their two cents.

The final conversation got Leonard and Betty to reflecting upon their lives. In many ways, this was for them the most important of the six conversations because it encouraged them to open up about how they saw themselves as people, describe how they had grown up, how they had met each other, and to tell about their life's journey and what matters to them. From this, the idea was launched to set down their story and the history of the family farm in writing as a "memory book." Then their daughter Allison, who holds a degree in film from the University of North Carolina, ran with the idea and suggested videotaping her parents as they shared their thoughts and feelings and strolled down memory lane. This could be a *living* memory book for grandkids and future generations to experience. Though a bit uncomfortable at first about going on camera, Leonard and Betty soon warmed to the idea, and in the end Allison wound up recording more than ten hours of legacy conversations with her father and mother. She eventually edited the footage down to a forty-five-minute documentary that she gave to her folks and to each of her siblings on videocassette as Christmas gifts. She also saved all the outtakes so that none of this permanent record of her parents' legacy conversation would be lost.

Maybe Not the Be- and End-All, but Wow!

The upshot of conducting these six conversations using the CARE system was that after years of difficulty communicating with each other, of family tension due to misunderstandings, and (on Leonard's part especially) of not feeling appreciated or listened to, the Wilson family had finally absorbed a lot of information about themselves, about each other, about family dynamics, and about how much they really mattered to one another. Most important, they knew where to go in terms of laying out an effective strategy for Leonard and Betty's long-term care (see part 3) and in continuing to strengthen their relationships with each other as well.

Will this mean an end to all family disagreements? No, of course not. Between family members—especially strong-willed people such as Leonard Wilson and his son Ben—there will always be disagreements. But in the Wilsons' case, there is now a strong bond of communication to mitigate such quarrels. How powerful is that!

So, let's not delay any longer. Let's proceed to the first important conversation, the big-picture conversation, and learn how to help you help your parents uncover the challenges, alternatives, and resources that exist in their particular situation, and to focus on the big picture regarding the experience they want for their long-term future care.

PART TWO

The Parent Care
Conversations

*There are two barriers that often prevent
communication between the young and their elders.
The first is middle-aged forgetfulness of the fact that
they themselves are no longer young. The second is
youthful ignorance of the fact that the middle-aged are
still alive.*

—Jessamyn West, novelist

3

The Big-Picture Conversation

The best way to predict the future is to invent it.

—Dr. Alan Kay, Hewlett Packard Labs

A Process Problem

In addition to the emotional obstacles holding us back from dialoguing with our parents or with our children about the parent care issue that I have already discussed in previous chapters, there is another culprit at work—arguably the biggest culprit of all. It is the fact that that we throw ourselves off balance by putting the cart before the horse. Let me explain.

Most elder adults really *do* want to talk to their spouses and children about their future care and all the issues related to it, but they don't know how. Neither, in most cases, do spouses or kids know how to begin such a dialog. This is because the major industries and service professions involved in parent care focus almost exclusively on a product-oriented approach to opening the discussion and addressing the problem. That approach can be, and all too often is, a nonstarter.

Typically, the legal, financial services, insurance industry, or CPA approach to parent care begins (and ends) with pitching a product that purportedly will solve part, or all, of the parent care problem. For example, a lawyer will tell you the solution is to make out a will, or perhaps, set up a trust, or employ some other legal tool that will protect your parents' assets, enrich their beneficiaries (that's you), and create an extension of their legal rights through general or health care powers of attorney.

❖ Reality Check

Parental Myth: "I have it all figured out and know *exactly* what I want to do. I've talked to my professional advisors and have everything in order. I'm *certain* of it!"

Fact: Don't believe your folks have their future care all figured out and have started putting things in order unless you see it all figured out and in order—on paper. Take it with a grain of salt that they have consulted their professional advisors (assuming they have them) about anything. Most likely, they have not. And while they may express certainty about how to proceed, realize this: they are probably just as certain about that as they were about how to raise you. In other words, they are pretty much making it up as they go along.

The financial services industry approach is not dissimilar. Here, the discussion focuses on growth and income over pure growth, weighted against your parents' risk profile and sensitivity to market volatility, with the emphasis on preservation of capital for preserving purchasing power, and so on. The insurance industry approach is only minimally less confusing and off-putting. Here, the discussed solution typically revolves around long-term care costs, available assets, Social Security contributions, pension benefits, and the minimization of potential estate taxes with an artfully structured individual or second-to-die life insurance policy. Just choose the tool you want, let it work its magic, and when events dictate, be ready to reap the windfall.

Last but not least, there is the CPA approach, which is to focus on the various state and federal regulations that affect the purchase of investment and insurance industry products, and the tax ramifications of those decisions. This will spark a scintillating conversation about the use of qualified versus nonqualified monies, Social Security taxation potential, IRA withdrawal tax traps, and whether or not there will be a sunrise after the sunset of current estate tax legislation. Good grief, no wonder our parents put off having this discussion. It's enough to make their heads spin.

❖ Reality Check

Parental Myth: "There's no need to plan. The government will take care of us."

Fact: While government assistance (Social Security, Medicare, and Medicaid) does indeed offer an avenue of support for older Americans, it is fast becoming a less certain avenue. Who knows where these programs will be in a few years in terms of solvency and benefits? Government assistance should be relied on as a last resort, not as a primary means of care and support.

Don't misunderstand me. I'm not saying that these solutions are inappropriate for dealing with the parent care issue, just that they are inappropriate as openers to any discussion of the issue. Parent care is first and foremost a process issue, not a product one. In other words, it is first and foremost about the conversation itself. The challenges our parents face, the alternatives they have, the resources they possess, and the experience they want to have as they age: that determines the "how." Without this in-depth conversation, the "how" will be just another force-fed quick fix and a transitory one too.

Deep Support

In her book *The Support Economy,** Harvard Business School professor Shoshana Zuboff argues that what today's consumers (especially today's older consumers, the baby boomers and their parents) yearn for is not more product presentation but a set of relationships—a system of *deep support*—that will allow them to reach their personal goals of psychological self-determination. Her point is this: Today's consumers are swamped by choice, whether it's the sixty-three different models of SUV they can buy, the nine thousand separate mutual funds they can invest in, or the twenty-three different kinds of deep-dish pizza they can order. Choice is not the issue. The issue is that I want what I want when I want it, in the way I want, at the price I want it—*now.* In other words, the issue is about maximizing the *consumer experience* in relation to goals and desires as opposed to maximizing the *consumption of products* and therefore being affected by that consumption in unpredictable and unintended ways.

---

*With James Maxmin. New York: Viking Press, 2002.

The conversations in this book lay the groundwork for maximizing the consumer experience of deep support in the area of parent care. In fact, they are the *beginning* of that experience. Once you have determined the type of deep support desired and the type of deep support that can be provided (the structure) to create the experience, the selection of the various professional, financial, or investment products to support that structure and maximize that experience is no longer the driving decision but almost a fait accompli.

With that in mind, let's help your parents draw a big picture of where they want to be a few years from now in terms of maximizing the experience of their future care.

❖ TIP! Choose a Facilitator

The parent care conversations cover many critical areas. Without someone to keep the discussion organized and moving forward, it can get bogged down or turn into a free-for-all. Choosing a facilitator within the family should be approached the same way as borrowing money from a family member—with care. The facilitator should be someone everyone trusts, who is not only able to articulate his or her own positions clearly but is a superb listener capable of understanding and restating the positions of others just as clearly. He or she should be someone with a history of working well and building consensus with family members, who engages conflict with a feather duster and not a crowbar. Granted, it may be that no one in the family is able to fill this bill 100 percent, but in order for the parent care conversations to work smoothly and effectively, a preponderance of these characteristics should be apparent in whomever you choose.

The Big-Picture Conversation

The series of parent care conversations starts with what I call the big-picture conversation because it will give you an insight into the kind of future your parents would like to experience and therefore create. Their responses here will tell you two important things:

1. That they have thought about their future as it relates to this topic.
2. That they trust you enough to talk to you about it. If your parents have not, will not, or cannot bring themselves to think about their long-term care from a conceptual standpoint, you have a huge challenge ahead of you. If they cannot or will not trust you enough to discuss the view they have, then you have an impossible task. *You cannot participate in or be held responsible for your parents' care unless you are a part of the conversation about that care.*

With that in mind, let's apply the CARE "hear and now" listening system to the big-picture conversation and see what results. Remember, the fundamental premise of CARE is that if people have a formula for organizing their thoughts around a subject, they will feel more comfortable about venturing forth and discussing that subject. CARE provides that formula for you and your parents.

1. CHALLENGES
"Mom and Dad, let's look down the road at the issue of your long-term care and discuss what you think are some of the biggest challenges you will face."

The idea here is to uncover whatever is preying on their minds about their future. Typically, what will emerge from the responses you get is an expression of overall panic, from many different angles, at the prospect of losing control over their future.

From the responses you get to this question, a big picture will emerge of the concerns and outright fears your parents have about their future and the issue of care in particular. Only when these challenges are spelled out will your parents begin to see the various options that exist to address them.

My experience is that there are at least ten big-picture challenges most parents say they face; maybe yours will add to this list:

- "How do we talk about this with our children without making them feel responsible for us?"
- "How can we get the children to work together on this instead of fighting with each other like when they were kids?"
- "How do we downsize and organize all our belongings without feeling as though we're giving up everything?"
- "The subject is too complicated. How can we prepare properly if we don't understand?"
- "How do we simplify our financial and legal affairs so that, if the time comes, our kids can step in and make decisions for us?"
- "How do we stay independent for as long as possible without being a danger to ourselves or others?"
- "How do we make sure we don't end up all alone and forgotten?"
- "How do we face the fact that we may not have enough money to do everything required of us to plan ahead successfully?"

- "How will we avoid alienating the rest of our children if we entrust just one of them to carry out our wishes?"
- "Can't we just die here so our kids will just have to have us buried?"

❖ Reality Check

Parental Myth: "We'll just be burdening our children more if we share things with them."

Fact: Parents actually burden their kids more by tuning them out on this subject or stonewalling them. This is one area where kids are very happy having surprises thrust upon them. And once the parents are gone, it's too late for them to ease the burden by helping the kids sort things out.

❖ TIP! It's Not About You

Remember, the parent care conversations are about your parents' thoughts and feelings, not yours. If asked for your opinion or suggestions, politely decline. Say you will be happy to share your opinion or make suggestions but only after they have shared theirs with you. This helps to reinforce the trust they must feel that you are truly focused *on them.*

---

2. ALTERNATIVES
"Mom and Dad, let's discuss some of the options that you think might be available to you in dealing with the challenges we just discussed."

The goal here is to help your parents shift their focus away from what they fear they will lose by making a decision about their future care to what they stand to gain from making that decision if they maximize their options. It may take some digging to discover these options, but together you can do it. That's the whole idea of this conversation (and all the others in the book): to discover the alternatives that exist, *together.*

For example, some might be:

- "We can break each decision down into manageable steps and plan one step at a time so we feel less overwhelmed."
- "We can start laying the groundwork by doing some investigating without having to lay out any cash."
- "We can use this book to help us discover what issues we have regarding our future care."

❖ TIP! Beware Procrastination

Procrastination transforms potentially resolvable situations into eternal dilemmas incapable of resolution. Teenagers are masters of this game: whatever solution you propose is simply impossible or unworkable for a thousand different reasons. Behind this procrastinating lurks the fear of making a decision in the first place or of not making the one that is "totally right"; i.e., finding the perfect solution, which of course can't be found because it doesn't exist. Like teenagers, your parents really have just two big-picture alternatives to consider: (1) they can make a decision that, while perhaps imperfect, does take into account their wishes and what's important to them, or (2) they can default to a decision created in crisis mode with little or no regard to their wishes and what's important to them.

- "We can see if there is such a thing as a professional mediator in this field to help us work things through."
- "We can ask friends who have already gone through this problem about what they did; maybe we can learn from them."

3. Resources

"Mom and Dad, let's think of some resources that you are familiar with already that we could use to help maximize your options and minimize these challenges."

Once your parents know the alternatives that exist to meet the challenges they face, they will be better able to put a name to the resources available to help with each alternative. In this and the five parent care conversations to come, your parents will discover more resources available than they would have ever thought existed. For example:

- "Get some basic information from our lawyer (CPA, banker, insurance agent, investment advisor) to help us map out a plan. Then hire them later to execute our desires for us."
- "Bounce ideas off each other as husband and wife, just as we've done throughout our married life."
- "Look at our children as adults who can and want to help us instead of continuing to look at them as kids whom we must shield."
- "Turn to our priest (pastor, rabbi) to help us think through some of these issues."
- "Start checking with our realtor to see what houses in this area, and others we might like, are going for now."

- "Visit some retirement communities and other types of care facilities to help us better understand the decisions we may be faced with."
- "Get a realistic view of where we stand financially."

Now that you have helped your parents to examine their challenges and consider their alternatives and resources, it is time to get them to imagine the experience they would like to create for themselves out of the decisions they will make.

4. EXPERIENCE

"Mom and Dad, think about the long-term care experience you would ideally like to create for yourselves and tell me what that experience would look like."

Perhaps more than any other question, your parents may need some prompting here to get going. This, after all, is a difficult question to answer even if one has been considering the prospect of one's future care for some time; it calls upon parents to contemplate having made decisions about their future care they have not yet made and to imagine the good they want to come out of them, so they will feel confident about moving toward making those decisions. However, by having vented freely about the "dark side" of growing older early on in the process, your parents will begin to see, and to articulate, the upside of the experience they can create for themselves.

For example:

- "We're able to breathe again because our heads are not in the sand."
- "We've thought everything through and resolved things and are free of dread."

- "We've brought our children into our confidence and aren't stressed about having to ask them to help us."
- "Thinking through where we might have to live eventually, and why, has actually enabled us to find ways to be able to stay where we are longer."
- "We've come to a good understanding with our children so that our expectations of each other are realistic."
- "We were able to stretch our finances because we started looking at ways to rearrange and improve them early enough."

From typical responses to the experience question such as these, your parents will be able to develop a list of positives that will help spur them to take action. I call these positives "experience accelerators," and some of them related to the big picture might be:

- "Making decisions now in anticipation of future events will help to us to build confidence about the future."
- "Just being able to hire someone to come in and help inventory and distribute some of our personal property removes all that complexity that clutter adds to our lives."
- "Making sure our legal affairs are in order now will give us the flexibility and adaptability to make changes later on as we need to."
- "Designating someone to help assist with health care decisions removes all the uncertainty that comes from not having anyone in charge."
- "Taking control of our finances will let us realistically determine what we have and what we need so that we won't be stressed out by the unknown."
- "Making decisions instead of avoiding them will restore balance to our personal and business affairs in such a way

that we will be able to confront the issue of care in a less forbidding context."
• "Just thinking through the various pieces involved in making long-term care decisions will help us to focus better on what's really important *to us*."

These accelerators, when set down on paper in black-and-white, will help to put your parents in a positive frame of mind with regard to making decisions about their future—whether the actual move on those decisions will be made a month from now or a year from now.

Granted, some of the sample responses I've provided may give the impression of flowing a little too easily. They may even appear a bit too simple and straightforward given the complex nature of the questions themselves. But I can assure you that while many parents may have the care issue on their minds, they will very likely not have come up with many solutions to that issue, let alone simple and straightforward ones. By asking them the big-picture questions, you get the ball rolling. You give them structure for envisioning what's most important to them in the years they have left and how to achieve it.

❖ **Keep in Mind!**

You may adapt the CARE questions to your own conversational style if it will make you feel more comfortable. Stay consistent, however, from conversation to conversation, and in order to elicit the information you need, be sure to maintain the essence of the questions as presented here.

Off and Running

Robert Meyer, seventy-two, and his wife Elizabeth, seventy-one, have each been retired for about ten years. They live in Boise, Idaho, where Robert had a very successful career as an executive at Bendix Corporation. They have two grown children, Kate and Zachary, both happily married with families of their own. Living in Denver and Salt Lake City, respectively, the children are close enough to make frequent trips home for the holidays and to pop in for the occasional visit with the grandkids as well.

The Meyers' son Zachary, having recently attended a parent care conversation seminar, suggested to his parents that they meet with their life insurance agent to talk about their future plans and the issue of long-term care. Zachary participated in the meeting as well. Initially, Robert thought the agent was just going to make a pitch for long-term care insurance or picking up more life insurance coverage. But the agent had attended the seminar also and was well versed in the CARE system. Instead of launching into a product pitch, the insurance agent surprised Robert and Elizabeth by asking them to share their feelings about the challenges they saw ahead of them surrounding the issue of their future care.

Robert and Elizabeth had never thought about long-term care as something they could actually *anticipate* and thus *plan for.* They had always felt, "We'll just deal with it all when the time comes." As they thought about this, they realized there were a number of things that concerned them. For example: What do we do with the house? Should we move to a retirement community? What kinds of things should we look for in choosing one? What kinds of care will we need? What in the world will we do with all our stuff ?

Zachary absorbed his parents' responses to the agent's question, then asked them to share with him and the agent some of the options they could think of that might be available to help them deal with these issues. Neither Robert nor Elizabeth had thought about their future in terms of options. They had simply figured the path was preordained, with little room for innovation. But their son's question got them to thinking broadly. Maybe they could build a smaller, stand-alone house. Or, even more exciting, perhaps they could buy into a "retire cruise," a new time-share concept for retirees wherein you purchase a half-interest in a condominium for use half the year. But this condominium is onboard a ship, making it sort of a floating townhouse.

Next, the insurance agent jumped in again and asked them for some of the resources they thought they might be able to tap to help maximize their options. Through years of saving and investing, the Meyers had put themselves in the position of not having to worry about money. They weren't wealthy, but they were very well-off. That was one resource they had on their side—a big one.

The fact that their physical health was so good was another huge resource they could tap. It meant they didn't need assisted living or special care considerations, at least not yet.

Their relationship with their children was yet another huge resource. Both kids said they would welcome it if their parents moved closer for even more frequent holiday get-togethers and "pop ins" with the grandkids.

Robert and Elizabeth Meyers' social skills and adaptability were another big asset. They had always found it easy to settle in and make new friends wherever they went.

Finally, Zachary asked his folks to paint for the insurance agent a picture of the future they would like to have as a result of the care decisions they would make. It was this question, the hardest for them to answer, that pushed Robert and Elizabeth to get in touch with their vision about what getting older really meant to them. It made them consider what they wanted to experience more, rather than less of, as the years wore on and what they could realistically hope to achieve to make those years fulfilling.

They said they wanted to feel unafraid of the consequences of their decisions. They wanted to experience self-sufficiency and independence for as long as realistically possible. And they wanted to stay connected to each other and to their family as they aged—in other words, to grow old, as they described it, "naturally."

When the meeting finished, Robert and Elizabeth realized they had never contemplated the issue of their future care before in such a comfortable yet pointed manner. They had always dreaded the subject. But the meeting had gotten them to imagine how they wanted their lives to look in the near future, and to share that vision with their son and the insurance agent so that they could help them bring that picture to life. Previously, the insurance agent had always talked to them only about product and policy decisions. This time was different. This time the discussion was just about them. That didn't mean the agent didn't have any insurance product or policy ideas up his sleeve. But now when the pitch came, there would be a context for it that hadn't existed before, and the product and policy suggestions would be in full alignment with the Meyers' long-term care goals and desires.

What Robert and Elizabeth Meyers saw from having the big-picture conversation was that they could actually shape the future they wanted for themselves as they grew older instead of defaulting to a series of circumstances that were "just meant to be." It would take some hard thinking and imagination on their part to design that future, but they were now ready to start.

Having begun to find the sense of confidence they needed to begin planning for and making decisions about their future care, Robert and Elizabeth were eager to launch into the other parent care conversations with their son. Zachary called his sister Kate, and with that call, the entire Meyers clan was off and running—talking openly, communicating fully, and planning together, strategically. *Just as you too will be able to do.*

4

The Money Conversation

"Blissfully" Unaware

Herb and Martha Pennington retired nearly ten years ago from the university where they had worked for most of their lives. Herb, a professor of biology, is a private man who, while open and affectionate with his wife and children, has always been very secretive on the subject of money. His father had died in bankruptcy, and, perhaps as a result of that experience, Herb became very frugal, determined to never let himself fall into that trap.

As a young professor, Herb struggled to support his mother, his wife Martha, and their two children, and yet he managed to put away a little each pay period to begin building a small portfolio of rental properties near the university. He kept them in his name alone because he didn't want his wife to be responsible should anything happen to him before the mortgages were paid off. He now had ten such properties, all mostly paid off, and the rental income from them was meant to help subsidize his and Martha's retirement income.

Martha, a former professor in the theater department, had inherited a small amount ($100,000) from her late mother, which she had given to Herb to take care of since he seemed to be so good at finances. The couple also had some life insurance through the university as well as a long-term care policy purchased elsewhere. With their home owned free and clear, the rental income, and two pensions coming in, Herb felt that he and his wife were in a good position to enjoy the fruits of their lifetime of work.

❖ Reality Check

Parental Myth: "We have enough money in our investments to be able to live forever just off the interest."

Fact: Here's a quick way to see if that's true. Take the total amount of money your parents have in their investment portfolio and multiply it by 3 percent. If that 3 percent meets their current living expenses, they may be right. If it doesn't, and their portfolio isn't earning at least 3 percent a year in interest, then they are in big trouble.

Recently, however, Herb was diagnosed with first-stage Alzheimer's and late-stage dementia. His son, an accountant, had for some time prior to the diagnosis attempted to talk with Herb about his finances, just to get a handle on where things were in the event something like this happened. But no matter how delicately Herb's son tried to broach the subject, the man begged off or changed the topic. Now, with his father's diagnosis of early Alzheimer's, the son was sure that if he didn't do something immediately, his parents (and possibly he as well) would be in serious financial jeopardy. The family physician had confided in him that Herb could probably expect to be able to live at home another year or so but due to the progression of the disease would likely have to go into an assisted-living situation directly after that because of the twenty-four-hour nature of the care that would be required.

Approximately a year after the initial diagnosis, Herb suffered a stroke that left him unable to communicate or to walk without assistance. With great pain and reluctance, but unable to care for him by herself any longer, his wife moved Herb to Cedar Village, an assisted-living center nearby, where she could at least visit him regularly. Cedar Village is a *complete* assisted-living center, which meant that it offered the possibility of transitioning Herb to a special care unit within the same facility if his situation required it.

The monthly cost of Cedar Village was $4,500, not including the medicine Herb required daily, which added another $450 to the monthly tab. It was now that Herb's son discovered that his father's retirement income plus Social Security came to $3,200 a month, almost $1,800 short. He further discovered that the long-term care policy his father had purchased to supplement any shortage only paid benefits for six months, at the rate of $50 per day, *if Herb was in an acute nursing facility.* Assisted living did not qualify as acute nursing.

Herb's son then looked to the rental properties to see if he could divert some of the monies to help subsidize his dad's care. The ten properties were bringing in a total of $2,400 a month. A believer that a bird in the hand is worth two in the bush, his father had not raised the rent in many, many years. In addition to the properties being underrented, the son discovered that they required a huge amount of maintenance, much of which had long been deferred: paint jobs, gutters, roofs, and carpeting that needed replacing, and so on. When he estimated the amount all this would cost, the total equaled 25 percent of the value of the properties. Understandably, the tenants were none too happy about the conditions they were living in and had banded together to withhold their rent as a protest. One tenant had even sued Herb over this, but because he was suffering from late-stage dementia, Herb had simply filed the letter away and forgotten about it.

When Herb's son combined the amount of money it would take to bring the properties up to a salable condition plus the tax bite incurred in selling them, the amount came to almost 40 percent of the properties' value. It was a complete between-a-rock-and-a-hard-place, rob-Peter-to-pay-Paul scenario.

Too fragile and upset over her husband's illness to remain in the family home, Martha decided to sell it and purchase a smaller, more manageable place. Her son estimated that she would realize $250,000 from the sale, all of it tax free. The smaller home she found cost $150,000. That left $100,000 that could be used to subsidize her husband's care because her own monthly pension and Social Security income were barely enough to cover her expenses.

Herb's son estimated the $100,000 would be gone in four to five years. For his father to be able to remain in Cedar Village after that, and to avoid having to go on Medicaid (and perhaps be moved somewhere else), the $100,000 had to last as long as possible. Therefore, he put it in the safest, risk-free-rate-of-return investments available to help the money grow. Herb's son also sold the rental properties at an "as is" loss and added the small amount of cash realized from the sale to the investment pot for his father's care.

As of this writing, Herb's Alzheimer's has progressed to the point where he must be moved to the special care section of Cedar Village, where his average monthly expenses will rise to about $7,200. Most of the $100,000 is gone; there is just enough left to cover Herb's expenses in the special care section for about a year. For his wife to be able to preserve some cash of her own and not see it all go to her husband's care, leaving her with nothing to live on, the only option is for Herb to move, after the year is up and the $100,000 gone, to a facility that accepts Medicaid payments. When that happens, of course, the State of Illinois will want whatever assets may be left over in Herb's estate as reimbursement for any monies it has spent on his care. Furthermore, given the new "look back" rules for Medicaid, the State of Illinois has the ability to go back nearly five years to determine reimbursements; it can investigate whether Herb had gifted his wife and children any money during this time that might in the future have been used for Herb's care. If the state determines those gifts were made in order to "defraud" the State of Illinois, Herb's wife and children could be forced to pay all that gifted money back, with interest, as well as face civil and perhaps criminal charges and fines.

❖ Reality Check

Parental Myth: "Our portfolio is doing well enough; we can buy our way into a nursing home when the time comes."

Fact: What if there are no beds available at that time in the nursing home your parents *want*, assuming they haven't outlived their money in the meantime and made the possibility of choice moot?

The one blessing of Alzheimer's, of course, is that Herb himself is "blissfully" unaware of any of this.

A Private Affair

So, how does a smart university professor like Herb Pennington wind up putting himself, his wife, and his son in such a financial noose? By not sharing his financial situation and not doing it early on.

The fact of the matter is that unless you know what assets your parents have and where those assets are, you won't be able to arrange things to maximize their use and to protect those assets as much as possible while not running afoul of the myriad federal and state Medicare and Medicaid rules and regulations. Not only will your parents not have any money to pass on to you, but you may end up facing financial ruin by having to subsidize their care out of your own income and investments pocket or be responsible for reimbursing the state for what it has paid out. The money conversation is your first line of defense against these scenarios.

Money is not the easiest topic to talk about with parents. They probably kept you out of that discussion while you were growing up, and it may be a difficult habit for them to break now. This is especially true of parents who grew up during the Great Depression. They belong to a generation with an emotional hangover from the worst financial disaster in our country's history (so far). For many people of that generation, there will never be enough of anything to make them feel totally secure financially. They will likely take their fear of growing old without money, a place to live, or enough food on the table with them to the grave. Money to this generation is a private issue—talked about in private, counted in private, and given away in private.

Another source of reluctance on the part of parents to talk about money with their adult children (or most other family members and friends for that matter) is that in the United States especially we tend to measure success in life almost solely by the amount of money we have accumulated during that life. Your parents may feel that they have not done well enough and be embarrassed to share that with you. Or they may feel that they have done so well that if they gave you a peek at what you might inherit then you would quit your job, throw caution to the wind, build up inventories of tanning oil and sun glasses, and generally join the ranks of the world's ne'er-do-wells.

For whatever reason your parents' financial status has been closed to you, your job now is crack open that door with the money conversation and gather the following critical information:

- How much in cash and other assets do your parents *actually* have?
- How much do they owe and to whom?
- How well is your parents' money working for them?
- What's not working about their money?
- What changes need to be made to correct that?
- What's possible and what isn't?

You will gather this information in two phases. The first is the money conversation itself, where you will use the CARE system to get at the more emotional issues your parents have concerning money and their financial situation. The answers you get here will enable you to dig deeper and collect the specifics about their financial situation and where their assets are located. In order to do this, you will need the latest statements from their bank(s), brokerage firm(s), insurance company (or companies), and so on. Once you have these statements, you will be able to record such information as asset location, title, account numbers, ownership, and other details. You need to have the most complete picture possible of where your parents are financially *right now.*

Having that picture is vital because your parents cannot begin to select a care facility—whether it is a retirement home or nursing home—until they understand what they are able to pay on a monthly basis for that facility and for how long. They and

---

❖ TIP! When Lips Are Sealed Tight

If you are dealing with parents who are in complete denial about their financial situation and are totally unwilling to discuss this aspect of their lives with you, you have two options. The first is to acknowledge that this is a smoke-screen, offer to help them organize their affairs, and try to get them to see that without knowing what they have, what they will need, and what they want, you may not be in a position to help them when the time comes. The second option is to exit stage left. Yes, I did say "exit." Parent care responsibilities are so huge, so draining, that if your parents aren't willing to meet you even halfway on the money issue, then they will simply have to live with the financial consequences of their noninvolvement. And you will at least have a heads-up that their finances are probably in poor condition, so you can prepare for the fallout from their default decision.

you won't know whether the family home is an asset or a liability, whether the amount of Social Security income they receive can be treated as "mad money" or if it must be depended upon. They won't know whether they can afford to give away that Rembrandt or if they'll have to sell it for hard cash to live on. Your parents didn't accumulate all they have in one night, so understand that you aren't going to grasp their financial picture in one night either.

The Money Conversation

1. CHALLENGES

"Mom and Dad, let's discuss some of the financial challenges you think are ahead of you with regard to long-term care."

What you are trying to get straight to with this question is whether your parents feel confident about their financial situation (and why) or whether the uneasiness they may be demonstrating about even discussing the subject is an attempt on their part to mask a deep anxiety they feel over their money situation. Here is how some of the responses might go:

- "We think we have enough for our future care, but we're not sure and don't know how to find out."
- "Our money is scattered in several banks and investment firms. We don't have a fix on where it all is ourselves."
- "We don't know if our assets are earning enough for us to be able to live the way we will want to and still be able to leave you kids something."
- "We don't know what to do or where to invest our money to make it grow to what we'll need."

- "We know how much we have, where it all is, and have organized and planned everything out. We'll show you."

Wow! If you get this last response, thank the gods who run the universe that you were born into your family, and spend your life working on world peace or world hunger, because you've just freed up the next twenty years!

2. ALTERNATIVES
"Mom and Dad, let's discuss some of the options that you think might be available to you in dealing with the financial challenges we just discussed."

Your parents may need some nudging here, particularly if they are in denial or unaware that there may be a problem with their money situation. If so, they may find it difficult to consider their options. Here are some of the options I've heard expressed:

- "Cross our fingers and just hope for the best."
- "Organize our affairs to find out where we stand."
- "Maximize the financial potential of what we have."
- "Find other sources of income or make our money grow."
- "Keeping making our own financial decisions about our current and future care."
- "Enlist our children's help to determine our financial picture and prospects."

This last type of response is an open invitation to proceed directly to the fact-finding part of the money discussion before moving on to the final two CARE questions. If you decide to finish the conversation before moving on to the fact-finding, that's OK too. It will all depend upon how well you "read" your parents: sometimes it's best to strike while the iron is hot.

If you do proceed to fact-finding, use the fact-finding tool below to record the pertinent financial data on your parents that you will need later on for analysis, strategizing, and decision making.

❖ TIP! Easy Does It

The process of gathering financial information from your parents can go smoothly or it can be frustrating and maddening, depending upon how you approach it. To achieve the first result, proceed in a way that is open and invitational, not judgmental. You don't want to cause your parents to feel any embarrassment. For example, don't go after the facts about their cash flow and investments like the cops on TV's *Law & Order*.

---

3. RESOURCES

"Mom and Dad, let's think of some financial resources that you are familiar with already that we could use to help you maximize your options and minimize the effect of these challenges."

The purpose of this question is to start your parents (and you) on the road to thinking about financial strategies, such as: how to transform current wealth into different assets and income streams; how to combine those streams and assets in a way that will maximize return (plus growth as well, if possible) while minimizing risks; and how to ensure that their money lasts as long as they do (with some left to be passed on to their beneficiaries). Coming up with a list of resources that can be tapped to help in the strategizing process is a key step, and the

Parent Care Solution Financial Fact-Finding Tool

	Value	Location
Cash on hand	_____	_____
Checking accounts	_____	_____
Certificates of deposit	_____	_____
Money market accounts	_____	_____
Stock mutual funds	_____	_____
Bond mutual funds	_____	_____
Individual stocks	_____	_____
Individual bonds	_____	_____
Annuities	_____	_____
Cash value life insurance	_____	_____
Gifts	_____	_____
Real estate equity	_____	_____
Art	_____	_____
Antiques	_____	_____
Jewelry	_____	_____
Rare coins	_____	_____
Collectibles	_____	_____
Heirlooms	_____	_____
Profit sharing plans	_____	_____
SEP	_____	_____
SIMPLE	_____	_____
401(k)	_____	_____
Other qualified pension plan(s)	_____	_____
Loans	_____	_____
Reverse mortgage	_____	_____
Line of credit	_____	_____

Total Assets: $ _____

number of such resources is probably limited only by your parents' imagination.

Broadly speaking, these resources may include people such as your parents' accountant, attorney, realtors, banker, and broker plus financial resources such as cash, stocks, bonds, real estate, business interests, pensions, retirement funds, and so on.

❖ Keep in Mind!

Don't forget that family itself can be a huge resource to leverage in this situation. I helped subsidize my father's care for nearly five years. It's easy to complain about having to do it, of course, but when you begin to feel that way, consider this: Add up the cost of caring for you for the first eighteen years of your life, plus all those times afterward that you needed (and got) that "little extra" to help tide you over until payday, catch up on your credit card debts, or take care of unexpected house or auto repairs. Only after the amount you have shelled out to help subsidize your parents' care begins to exceed the amount they shelled out for you for those eighteen years or longer will you really have some cause to complain.

---

4. EXPERIENCE

"Mom and Dad, think about the long-term care experience you would ideally like to create for yourselves as a result of the financial decisions you will have made, and tell me what that experience would look like."

What you are striving to come up with here is the ideal picture of your parents' future care situation, fiscally speaking, *from their point of view.* In other words, as if money were not an obstacle. Here are some of the responses to this question I have heard:

- "We would like to know that we have enough money to stay in our home and live a normal life without worrying about food or necessities until we absolutely have to move."
- "We would like not to be a burden on anyone, especially our children."
- "We would like to know that we would not have to live in lesser circumstances or experience a lower quality of life and care than we have now."
- "We would like to know that we can live out our lives in dignity, with as much autonomy and independence as is humanly possible."
- "We would like to know that if we do run out of money, caring for us will not drain the coffers of our children or our community."

For some parents, of course, approximating this picture will require coming up with millions of dollars a year in income or assets. For others, it will require as little as the cost of the least expensive compact car, in terms of their net worth. With your fact-finding completed and everything now out on the table, you are ready to help your parents find out which column they come closest to falling into, and how to begin planning for, and creating, the experience they desire.

Developing Money Planning Strategies

Keeping Principal Intact (as Much as Possible)
What you are trying to do in this chapter is get a feel for how long your parents will be able to sustain themselves in a facility (by which I mean their current home as well as any future retirement community, assisted-living, special care, or acute care situation) without:

1. Beginning to deplete the principal on their assets
2. Going completely broke and losing all control over their future care situation while saddling you and/or the government with the bill

To find these things out, you will need to calculate how much your parents will be able to safely withdraw from their assets over time.

There is scads of financial software available to help you and your parents assess their portfolio under a multitude of scenarios, conditions, and factors. While perhaps this might be an interesting exercise from an intellectual standpoint, and even fun from the point of view of "financial planning as a video game," in the end you will still be left with the following question: where do things stand now and where will they stand tomorrow?

As a result of conducting the fact-finding expedition earlier, you may already have a fix on where your parents stand now in terms of their total assets (the principal). If not, now is the time to find out, using the fact-finding tool. After that, get a rough fix on the second part of the question—how much your parents can withdraw over time without having to eat into principal—

under the following scenarios. For each one, base your calculation on the asset total you came up with using the fact-finding tool, coupled with the markets' average earnings-growth per annum over the past century; i.e., 9–10 percent.

• **Real-case scenario:** Total assets minus 50 percent of historical growth average, or 4–5 percent. This means your parents can withdraw 2–3 percent from earnings each year without eating into the principal. Bear in mind, however, that if the markets flatten out or go down (as happened, for example, from 2000 to 2004), then your parents will not be withdrawing from earnings but from the principal.

• **Worst-case scenario:** Total assets minus 100 percent of historical growth average. This means your parents' average 4–5 percent withdrawal per annum will be eating directly into their principal *right from the beginning.*

• **Best-case scenario:** Total assets minus 20 percent of historical growth average. In this case, your parents' portfolio will be growing in the range of 7–8 percent per year. They should plan on withdrawing no more than 4–4.5 percent to keep the principal intact.

Some analysts may consider these formulas to be overly simplistic. But having watched my father's life savings disappear in a four-year bear market, my level of assurance in the prognostications of most analysts is less than zero. The fact of the matter is that in the last years of a person's life the cost of care will equal almost 20 percent of that person's health care expenditures over his or her entire life up to that point. Any calculation based on assumptions about the future should always be considered with caution and common sense, of course. But the bottom line is that keeping things simple works. The name of the money planning game is fundamentally this:

1. Watch what your parents' money is earning.
2. Watch what your parents are spending.
3. When 2 exceeds 1, your parents are spending more than they are bringing in, a financial plan that is stressful on the family in the short term and catastrophic in the long term.

Conducting an *Easy Money–Hard Money Analysis*

Your parents' goal is to maximize both income and growth. At some point, they will have to turn the growth into some type of income to pay their bills. This is where what I call the "easy money–hard money" concept comes in.

Think of your parents' assets as breaking down in two different ways: easy money and hard money. Easy money assets are those that:

• Are easily accessible via a phone call, check, or debit card
• Are easily transferred from one account to another
• Produce little or no income tax liability from their use
• Do not affect long-term capital growth potential

Hard money assets are those that:

• Are difficult to convert to easy money
• Are not quickly or easily sold
• Have an income tax bill attached to their sale
• End the potential for long-term capital growth

The rule of thumb is that the closer an asset gets to being made of bricks and mortar, the more difficult liquidation of that asset becomes. Use the following Easy Money–Hard Money Decisions Tool to analyze which of your parents' assets is which and to determine how many months of care your parents' assets can sustain. Start by inserting the values you came up with earlier during your fact-finding expedition into the appropriate easy money or hard money column.

Conducting Your Analysis

Steps for easy money analysis
1. Total all the easy money amounts.
2. Divide the total by the amount required monthly.
3. Determine the number of months available.
4. Assume it doesn't earn anything.

Steps for hard money analysis
1. Total all the hard money amounts.
2. Divide the total by the amount required monthly.
3. Determine the number of months available.
4. Assume it doesn't earn anything.

The total number of easy money months plus total number of hard money months equals the total number of care years your parents' current financial picture will sustain. You will now know how hard your parents' portfolio must work to improve their long-term financial situation so that the experience they want can be realized.

Creating a Savings Account for Your Parents
The United States Congress is considering legislation to create what's called a Parent Care Savings Account (PCSA). This account, if created, would be a supplemental pretax savings account where a certain percentage of your paycheck or self-employment income could be used to supplement the payment

The Parent Care Solution
Easy Money–Hard Money Decisions Tool

Easy money		Hard money	
Cash on hand		Real estate equity	
Checking accounts		Tangibles	
Certificates of deposit		Art	
Money market accounts		Antiques	
Stock mutual funds		Jewelry	
Bond mutual funds		Rare coins	
Individual stocks		Collectibles	
Individual bonds		Heirlooms	
Annuities		Pension plan	
Cash value life Insurance		Profit sharing plans	
Gifts		SEP	
		SIMPLE	
		401(k)	
		Other qualified plan	
		Loans	
		Loans	
		Reverse mortgage	
		Line of credit	
Total easy money		Total hard money	

of medical and care expenses for your aging parents. If this leg-islation were passed, you would be able to add these amounts to your existing 401(k) contributions, profit sharing, or medical savings accounts monies for tax deduction purposes. The tech-nology already exists to allow PCSA contributions to be distin-guished from your normal contributions and thus be managed and accounted for separately.

These PCSA contributions could be used to supplement the care needs of your parents and any residual amounts could be rolled forward to pay for your own future care or that of your children or future generations. Not even the IRS should have a problem with this because if the PCSA-allotted monies are not used for care needs (substantiation may be requested), the IRS could levy early withdrawal penalties as well as onerous income taxes on the misspent funds.

Call your congressman and press for a vote, then stay tuned to my Web site (www.parentcaresolution.com) for the latest word on this potentially groundbreaking legislation.

Leveraging the Equity of the Family Home

The only thing that may be more sacred to Americans than the American flag is the family home. In chapter 6 ("The House Conversation"), I will explore many of the reasons for this, so I won't repeat them here. What I will do, since we are talking about money, is share with you my Parent Care Solution Home Equity Maximization Strategy for accomplishing just what the name of that strategy says, in order to keep the costs of parents' future care from causing them (and you) to go broke.

This strategy consists of two alternative steps:

1. Borrow the equity of the home to the maximum amount possible, and then place the equity in a single premium imme-

diate annuity. The payments from the annuity can fund the mortgage payment as well as provide income to the parents. A safety feature here is to add five years to the parents' mortality age (according to life insurance tables), and make sure that the annuity payments continue for at least that long. Another safety feature is to purchase credit life insurance on the mortgage or home equity line so that it is paid off completely upon the death of the parents. In this way, the parents receive income they can use to supplement their care, the loan is completely paid off when they die, and you get the money out of the house.

2. If parents don't need to use the equity from their house to borrow from and live on, then they can use part or all of it to purchase life insurance for the same purpose. Some caveats here. They should make sure that if they purchase a single premium policy (where a single lump sum payment is all that is necessary to carry the policy until they die), they use the most conservative assumptions possible in designing that policy. They don't want to put $100,000 in a $1 million life insurance policy only to find out ten years later that they need to put in another $250,000 to keep the policy from lapsing. Policy design is everything here. They (and you) should work with a professional insurance advisor, financial planner, or accountant in designing a policy. Don't be fooled by the illustrations on the brochure. The only thing the insurance company is obligated to pay for is what it is contractually obligated to in the fine print.

Protecting Assets, Privacy, and Inheritance

In the future, the funding requirements for Medicare and Medicaid will almost guarantee that federal and state governments will be looking for reimbursement of funds expended on behalf of the elderly. This reimbursement will come either from the assets of the person's estate or from assets that have been transferred to children in an attempt to avoid those assets being taken by the government. In fact, technology platforms are now in place with the ability to file constructive liens on the part of the state and federal government from the time of death until an estate is distributed, to recover monies expended on the part of the deceased. In some instances, states are pursuing the children of Medicaid-dependent parents to recover monies that were transferred in order to care for those parents.

It is important to understand here that deliberately and purposefully transferring assets or rearranging one's financial affairs with the intent of defrauding Medicaid is illegal and punishable by law. Nevertheless, every citizen does have a right to organize his or her financial affairs for the purpose of maximizing accumulated life's wealth and transferring as much as possible of that wealth to his or her children and community with a minimum amount of interference from the state or federal government.

I believe that if you design a comprehensive financial strategy with long-term goals of cash flow maximization, income tax reduction, investment planning, retirement maximization, and wealth-transfer (estate) planning, and if you review and update that plan periodically to accommodate changes in law and circumstance, not only will your plan help you accomplish your financial goals and objectives, but you will survive any scrutiny about transfers that occurred as part of that plan.

It is the responsibility of each of us not only to plan for our own financial success but also to be responsible for helping our parents continue to be successful in their older years. There will always be a percentage of our population that will not plan for anything: breakfast, career, vacation, or even its own well-being. But that percentage is undoubtedly not reading these words, which are not intended for them anyway. They are intended for those of you who are willing to take the responsibility and be accountable for the destiny of your parents' care and your own as well. For these reasons, it is important that asset protection, privacy protection, and inheritance-transfer planning be initiated as early as age sixty, which means *immediately* if your parents (or you) are now over sixty. Here's what to do:

1. Set specific goals, based on your easy money–hard money analysis, for the accumulation your parents will need so that they can start setting aside those amounts now. The savings can come from a salary, part-time job, or other sources of revenue. If the analysis says that your parents will not have enough without financial support from you and other sources, no matter what they do, the answer is not to surrender to a default solution *but for them to do the best with what they have.* There are only two variables to consider: income and expenses. If there's too much expense and not enough income then the options are to decrease the expense or to create more income while keeping the expense constant.

2. Take advantage of all legal structures and documents (see part 3) available for safeguarding assets, privacy, and the transfer of wealth. Furthermore, consult with an elder care attorney well-versed in the intricacies of Medicaid and Medicare law to enable your parents to protect as many of their assets as possible while still complying with the letter of the law. For a list of such attorneys throughout the country, visit the National Academy of Elder Law Attorneys Web site at www.naela.com.

Avoiding Medicare and Medicaid Pitfalls

Medicare and Medicaid planning reminds me of those commercials on television where you see a driver in a hot car careening down a scenic but precarious mountain road and a disclaimer flashes on the screen saying, "closed course, professional driver—

do not attempt this with your own vehicle." If your analysis shows that your parents are or may be candidates for governmental assistance for their future care, it is *critical* to seek out an estate and elder law attorney who specializes in this area. Medicare and Medicaid are complicated systems that are constantly undergoing governmental changes, and their application varies from state to state. But here are the basics.

People sometimes confuse Medicare with Medicaid. Yes, both are programs for the elderly, but Medicare pays for the costs of hospitalization and medical care, not for long-term care in skilled nursing or assisted-living facilities. Medicaid pays for that. Also, Medicaid pays care providers directly and not the recipient, and it is a needs-based program, which, even though federal, allows the individual states to establish their own eligibility and administration standards. Be aware that not only do laws vary from state to state but offices within each state may have their own standards as well. Now you see why I emphasize the need for an attorney experienced at navigating this maze.

All applications for Medicaid have to be made with the appropriate state agency. Though each state will have different priorities, all require the following:

1. **Proof of Residency (and Citizenship)**
2. **Proof of Eligibility,** for which there are several qualifying tests:
   a. Category test: Applicants must be sixty-five years of age (or older) and in need of long-term care due to age, blindness, or physical or mental disability. A forty-year-old may qualify too, if he or she is blind or permanently disabled.
   b. Income test: Congress has established a minimum income, below which it believes no elderly American

should fall. This minimum is called the Social Security Income (SSI) standard, and it varies annually based on the consumer price index. The *maximum* amount of income an applicant can receive and still receive Medicaid is *three times* the SSI standard. Currently, that standard is $579 a month. Three times that would be $1,737 a month. There are some caveats here, however:

- Income for Medicaid purposes includes all money received on a *regular basis,* such as pensions and other retirement plan income, Social Security, and annuity payments.

- It may not matter if an applicant's income exceeds the current SSI standard for eligibility if the applicant lives in a "medically needy" state or in a state where excess income is not an impediment to qualification. Parents should contact their local Medicaid office to determine their state's eligibility standards.

- Income is separated according to whose name appears on it. This means that an applicant's income is attributed solely to him or her while all income in a spouse's name (called a community spouse) is attributed to both spouses. Income in both names is attributed equally to each spouse. In 1988, Congress passed the Medicaid Catastrophic Coverage Act (MCCA) to avoid impoverishing the community spouse due to the expenses of the other spouse needing care. This means that even if the community spouse's income is greater than the spouse applying for Medicaid, he or she does not have to share that income with the other spouse. But if the community spouse does not have sufficient income of his or her own to meet what's called the Minimum Monthly Maintenance Needs Allowance (MMMNA), then the community spouse may be entitled to some income from the spouse applying for Medicaid. Be aware that there are additional Medicaid provisions for hardship situations, as well.

c. Resource test: An applicant's assets are categorized as either exempt or countable. Here's how the distinction works:

- **Exempt Assets.** An applicant can own an unlimited amount of these, which include: a home (as long as the applicant, spouse, minor or disabled child lives there—be on notice however that the state may place a lien on it for reimbursement of expenses or to recover expenses from the estate of the applicant); an automobile (if used for employment or medical treatment transportation, if the vehicle has been modified specifically to meet the requirements of the applicant's particular circumstances, or if there is a spouse); household items (almost all furniture, furnishings, artwork, etc.); personal effects (usually subject to a $2,000 limit); medical equipment needed by the applicant or spouse; burial needs (funeral plot, vault, casket, headstone, plus money for expenses set aside in a burial fund or a life insurance policy of less than $1,500 in face value); tools (used for a trade or business); a maximum of $2,000 cash ($3,000 if both spouses apply).

- **Countable Assets.** These include everything that can be converted to cash but does not fall into the exempt category, such as: real estate (other than a home or if the home is held in a trust); retirement assets like IRAs, 401(k)s, or any other deferred compensation (While some states treat tax-deferred balances as exempt, most will look at whether the account owner could demand the balance. If so, the balance—minus any applicable tax liability—will be countable. There are exceptions for mandatory IRA distributions past age 70½ and for annuities with certain irrevocable elections made inside those plans); liquid or cash equivalents (checking and savings accounts, stocks, bonds, mutual funds, and cash value life insurance); promissory notes (land sales contracts and trust deeds, though "countability" will depend on whether there is a demand feature within the note).

· **Unavailable Assets.** These are assets that are not capable of being converted to cash—for example, real estate owned with someone else or unmarketable property owned with other parties. Applicants may be required to produce evidence from time to time to substantiate the unavailability of these assets.

❖ Keep in Mind!

The "resource test" becomes more complicated if only one spouse is applying for Medicaid benefits. Title to property is largely irrelevant here, since all "countable" assets will be pooled whether they are in the husband's name, the wife's name, or joint. The Community Spouse Resource Allowance (CRSA) under Medicaid law does provide some protections, so be sure to consult the attorney advising your parents about this.

"Spend Down" Strategies

Once an eligibility analysis of your parents' income and resources has been completed and their Medicaid qualification has been determined, the next focus is how to "spend down" certain assets. The intent here is not to defraud Medicaid but to enhance your parents' quality of life as well as to preserve other assets and income for transfer to family members and future generations. The viability of these strategies for "spending down" assets will vary depending upon whether you are dealing with one parent (single parent) or two (married parents), as follows:

- **Single Parent Strategies:** These strategies revolve around what do with countable assets in excess of $2,000.
    a. Purchase an annuity. This essentially converts a resource asset into an income asset, guaranteeing a consistent income stream from this source while at the same time letting other assets grow. This strategy will only work if the payout election period is certain and the recipient dies before that period ends. Otherwise, the state might attempt to recover any remaining unpaid payments. There are lots of traps for the unwary here, like excessive fees and charges, so beware of them (or make sure your advisor is). The annuity marketplace is fairly competitive and the costs are becoming more transparent, so don't overlook this "spend down" opportunity.
    b. Give half and keep half. Gifts have an effect on Medicaid eligibility. Gifts, per se, are not illegal. They may, however, affect the waiting period for benefits, sometimes called the "period of ineligibility" or "penalty period." Within certain parameters, there is an almost

unlimited gift exclusion to family members such as a minor child, spouse, permanently disabled child, sibling with an equity interest in the home, or an adult child living with and providing care for the parent. Otherwise, the strategy here is to give away a calculated amount while holding back enough to cover the cost of care until the waiting period expires.

c. Prepay funeral and burial expenses.

d. Pay off all debt and credit cards.

e. Liquidate qualified or tax-deferred plans (for example, IRAs, 401(k)s, etc.) and prepay the tax liability. If taxes will not create a whole new set of problems, the liquidation strategy should not be overlooked.

f. Hire family members to provide care. This strategy has to be pursuant to a written agreement between the parties, and the family member(s) receiving payments for care provided should know that these payments are *taxable income.*

g. Prepurchase medical equipment and supplies that will be needed.

h. Prepurchase consumer items the parent will need, such as clothing, a television, room decorations, magazine subscriptions, books on tape, and so on.

• **Married Parents Strategies:** A couple may "spend down" using all the same strategies as a single parent, plus some additional ones. For example, unlimited assets can be transferred between spouses without being counted as gifts. Here are some others:

a. Purchase a larger home.

b. Put money into an existing residence by either paying off the mortgage (if there is one) or making needed improvements.

c. Purchase exempt assets such as an immediate lump sum annuity. As long as the payout option is not changeable and the payments are not assignable, an annuity that pays a certain amount is exempt in many states. Yours could be one of them.

❖ **Keep in Mind**

As noted earlier in this chapter but well worth repeating here: All state agencies have a right under Medicaid law to "look back" five years into an applicant's financial affairs at gifts made to or from a trust to determine if the state should be reimbursed. Under Medicaid law, the "look back" period for gifts made by the applicant to individuals is 35 months.

Recovering Costs:
A Guaranteed Way Not to Go Broke

One of the most difficult challenges in caring for aging parents is coming to the realization that not only do they not have enough money to pay for the duration of their care, but they also do not have enough money to cover the *current* cost of their care. Children in this situation are faced with an incredibly difficult choice: to watch their parents spend themselves into insolvency or to step up to the plate and divert sorely needed savings and retirement plan contributions of their own in order to help their parents out. This is the classic "heads you lose, tails you lose" dilemma. But it can now be solved, allowing both parents and offspring to recover the confidence to move forward. Here's how.

My solution is called the Parent Care Cost-Recovery System, and it provides a viable alternative to the traditional "heads you lose, tails you lose" dilemma. It involves insuring the lives of parents with either an individual policy on each parent or a second-to-die policy on both parents. The owner of the policy can be the one paying the premiums or anyone else in the family who is contributing to the current support of Mom and Dad and may need to recover those costs. The beneficiary of the policy can be anyone the owner of the policy deems appropriate. The proceeds of the policy can first be used to pay back the monies spent for Mom and Dad's care, with the balance used to replace any inheritance that was lost due to the high costs of care incurred. In some instances, these proceeds will result in the creation of an estate and an inheritance where none previously existed. The benefits of using life insurance in this situation are that the insurance proceeds, if properly structured, arrive untouched, untaxed, on time, and guaranteed.

Some people have expressed a certain discomfort with this strategy because they see it as profiting from the parents' demise. But consider this: (a) buying a life insurance policy on your parents certainly doesn't create or hasten that demise, which is inevitable; (b) your parents I'm sure would rather that you recover whatever you've spent caring for them than go broke and have to pass your retirement and future care needs onto your own children.

The question to really keep asking yourself as you consider this strategy is not "Am I profiting from the death of my parents?" but "If my money is paying for my parents' care, whose money will pay for mine?" If you already have a trust fund, are really tight with a wealthy Auntie Mame, or have married into the Hilton family, then the question is moot. But for most of us, the Parent Care Cost-Recovery System is a sound and worthwhile alternative.

So, how do you go about the recovery? There are five steps:

1. Using the easy money–hard money and income/resources analyses you conducted with your parents, determine if you will need to contribute to your parents' care now or in the future.
2. Determine how much you will need to contribute and for how long.
3. Calculate the impact diverting these monies will have on your own retirement and future care needs.
4. Determine how you will pay for the insurance premiums used to recover these monies.
5. Determine who will own the policy and who will be the beneficiary (or beneficiaries).

The insurance industry is both creative and flexible in the types of policies it offers and the financing of them. For example, there are some insurance companies that will loan you the money for the premium payments on an interest-only basis. At your parents' death, you pay back the amount the insurance company has advanced plus any unpaid interest. If you cannot find an insurance company that will loan you the money to do this, then consider taking out a home equity or other bank loan, or look to your current cash flow capabilities, the sale of assets, or any combination thereof to pay for the premiums. But always remember: the strategy behind the Parent Care Cost-Recovery System is to leverage your cash flow as much as possible but not by going so deeply into debt that you negate the strategy's value. Stay focused not only on how you are going to help pay for your parents' care but also on how to ensure you will be able to sustain your own retirement and future care needs so that your children won't have to pony up for you.

Putting It All Together

Among several reasons for our avoiding the money conversation is this one: the fear of what we might find. It is possible that our parents aren't as well-fixed financially as we thought (or were led to believe), and since we may not be where we would ideally want to be either, this knowledge makes us feel as though we are about to experience a car wreck that we can do nothing to stop.

But here's another way to think about what the money conversation may reveal. It's not what we find out that's the problem; it's what we want to believe is true, and isn't, that is the problem.

The minute you have a realistic picture of your parents' financial situation, you can begin to help them alter that picture. Even if your parents have little or no prospect of creating another dime of income for their future care—and you are barely making ends meet yourself—a car wreck is not inevitable. There are government programs like Medicaid to step in and help. That's why those programs exist. But before your parents can take advantage of such programs, they must be able to demonstrate that they qualify for them by determining the exact status of their financial situation. It is avoiding the money conversation that truly puts your parents' future care and your fiscal future in harm's way. Here's how things should work.

Bob and Crystal Taylor are solid working-class folks living in Omaha, Nebraska, and have recently retired. Bob ran a small restaurant (Taylor's Tin Cup Diner) and Crystal was an English teacher in the Omaha public school system. Their daughter, Ashley, and her husband, Max, live in Kansas City, where Ashley is an executive secretary for the Kansas City Gas Company and Max owns and operates Max's Tire Emporium. Ashley and Max do very well financially and have no concerns about their own retirement and long-term care. But Ashley didn't really know what her parents' financial situation was; she could only speculate. She knew that while growing up she always had nice clothes, the family always took wonderful summer vacations, and that when she graduated from college she had no student loans to pay off. Her folks had even helped her and Max out with the down payment on their first home and then forgiven the note. Therefore, Ashley assumed they were financially OK. But just *how* OK? To find out, she engaged her parents in the money conversation.

During the course of that conversation, Ashley discovered that her parents had invested their money wisely. Her mother had more than $300,000 in her school retirement plan, plus $1,200 a month coming in from Social Security, and another $700 per month from a defined benefit program from an earlier job. In addition, Crystal's late grandmother had left her another $200,000, which has since grown to $420,000.

Ashley's father has $250,000 invested in his profit sharing plan, plus he owns the building his diner is in, which is worth approximately $450,000 and is debt free. Based on his earnings, he is entitled to almost $1,300 per month in Social Security income. Both parents carry $250,000 worth of life insurance. The family home is worth $325,000, with no mortgage debt, and they own their cars and have no consumer debt.

Ashley's parents shared with her that in a couple of years they would like to downsize to a smaller residence close to her, in Briarwood Retirement Community in Kansas City. To do this, they will purchase the smaller home for about $250,000 and pay cash for it, leaving them with about $50,000 for an emergency fund. By pooling their savings together, they can live comfortably on Social Security alone yet have access to almost $5,200 per month without eating into principal. This is as far as their thinking and calculations had taken them. But what about further down the road, when assisted living or acute care might be needed?

One of the things the money conversation revealed Bob and Crystal Taylor had not done, even though they had talked about doing it, was purchase long-term care insurance. Their daughter encouraged them to make an appointment with their insurance agent to discuss the matter, and she went along. It turned out that since her parents wanted to be sure they would have enough for their future care without assistance from anybody and yet still be able to pass on substantial assets to their daughter and grandchildren, long-term care insurance was an excellent investment for the couple. They committed to a policy for each of them.

The Taylors also made a commitment to meet with their lawyer and update their estate documents to take into account the purchase of long-term care insurance and other changes that had occurred since the documents were originally drawn up (when their daughter was a child). Even though these were basic documents, there was a need for updated health care directives and a redrafting of the Taylors' powers of attorney to name their grown daughter and her husband as dual holders of their powers of attorney. With just a few changes and some good strategizing, Bob and Crystal have now fully organized their affairs in such a way as to provide a maximum amount of financial security for themselves and a minimum amount of financial difficulty relating to their future care for their daughter and son-in-law. And everyone now feels a sense of confidence about what lies ahead financially. That confidence could only grow out of having the money conversation, not by avoiding it.

❖ DOs and DON'Ts

DO make sure you know exactly where your parents are financially.

DO make sure you know where all of their financial assets are located.

DO know the names of your parents' accountant, attorney, and banker, and how to contact them.

DO estimate what it's going to take your parents to live on in their long-term care situation.

DO take responsibility for planning your parents' long-term care finances.

DON'T let your parents try to put off talking about money with you.

DON'T take their word for it that their finances are OK.

DON'T assume that someone else in the family will financially rescue them—or you.

DON'T bank on the government (or anyone else) providing all the necessary funds for your parents' long-term care.

DON'T wait until the s—t hits the fan to try to figure all this out.

5

The Property Conversation

Useless Appeal

There is an interesting corollary between personal property and sibling relationships. Both start out new and shiny. Over time, some wear occurs, resulting in little nicks. As the years pass, the nicks turn into cracks and the glue that once held everything together begins to yellow and harden and pull away. If enough stress is applied at a certain moment, the entire piece can crumble from the weight it has endured all these years. Time and circumstance have combined to create the ideal conditions for that collapse.

In the same manner, sibling relationships that have endured for years can suddenly be torn asunder by a picture, a hope chest, or a wedding ring that, in the stress of the moment that accompanies a parent's death, goes to "someone else." As a lawyer, financial advisor, and gatekeeper for families in the parent care area, I have seen this happen over and over again. Case in point: the Albright family of Albuquerque, New Mexico.

Bill Albright was the owner of Albright's Market, a combination convenience store and gas station. Bill had one of the largest collections of Anasazi pottery in the Southwest, having inherited part of it from his father, an amateur archeologist, and acquired the balance of it as a result of his own Saturday expeditions into the desert with his son, Bill Jr. Even though nothing was written down, Bill Sr. had indicated by his words and his actions that if something ever happened to him, then Bill Jr. was entitled to the pottery collection.

❖ Reality Check

Parental Myth: "The Salvation Army will take everything we don't want."

Fact: The Salvation Army and charities like it need clothing, furniture, and other articles that aren't subject to dry rot. They don't want Krugerrands, canned goods with a sell-by date of 1965, or clothing that went out of style when Bobby Darin died any more than you or anyone else in your family do.

Neva Albright, Bill Sr.'s wife, was an amateur painter and photographer. Neva had achieved national recognition for some of her photographs and paintings of the Southwest. At a showing in Santa Fe, the owner of a Washington, DC, gallery had bought nearly $50,000 of her work at wholesale for his own gallery. Dotty, one of Bill and Neva's two daughters, had always helped her mother organize and catalog her works. According to Dotty, Neva said that when something happened to her, Dotty could pick out what she wanted from the work and let her siblings have what was left to divide among themselves.

Neva Albright passed away four years ago, and her husband followed a year later. Their estate plan left everything to each other. The Albrights' attorney gathered the four children (Bill Jr., Dotty, Sam, and Elizabeth) together shortly after their father's memorial service to read his last will and testament. It was their father's intent to divide everything equally among the children, including bank accounts, the family home, personal property, and the convenience store. He had a clause in his will that said if they could not agree, the attorney would make the decisions, and they would have to abide by them. What happened next is the kind of nightmare that the property conversation is designed to circumvent.

The siblings went to their parents' home after the reading of

---

❖ Reality Check

Parental Myth: "There's not really all that much stuff. Your mother can sort through it and get rid of it quickly when the time comes."

Fact: Sure she can, beginning with the thirty-seven years of *Popular Mechanics* underneath the workbench in the garage, then the same-size piles of *Woman's Day, Redbook,* and *National Geographic* in the den. And those are just the magazines of which they accumulated the *fewest* issues!

the will. There, Sam asked Dotty and his brother if everything in the house had been left the way it was when their father died. Bill Jr. said that he had taken the pottery collection from the gas station since his father had promised it to him, and Dotty indicated that she had taken the photographs and paintings her mother had specifically given to her. Sam and Elizabeth got furious and began accusing their siblings of cheating them out of the chance to choose equally among this property, saying there was no hard evidence that either parent had singled things out for Bill Jr. or Dotty to take; the will alone controlled that. It did not help the situation that the spouses of all the parties were also present. A shouting match followed that resulted in Sam and his wife, and Elizabeth and her husband, storming from the house, vowing to "get a lawyer and make sure we get what we're supposed to."

Sam and Elizabeth felt the pottery collection and the paintings and photographs possessed as much monetary as sentimental value, if not more. They were concerned that their siblings had "cherry picked" the estate of the most valuable assets and thought that, therefore, they were entitled to an equivalent amount—in dollars if not in property itself. Their attorney sent a letter to Bill Jr. and Dotty, demanding that they immediately return the objects they had taken or provide an appraisal of those objects and send the equivalent in cash. The appraisal value of the pottery collection in Bill Jr.'s possession and the artwork in Dotty's home was in excess of $200,000. When their siblings received this news, they got even more furious and accused Bill Jr. and Dotty of cheating them by manipulating their father and mother.

Negotiations quickly broke down. Bill Jr. and Dotty refused to relinquish control of either the pottery or the artwork, citing their belief that their parents wanted them to have these things and that the "divide equally" clause in the will meant to divide everything that was *left*. Sam and Elizabeth were equally adamant, claiming that not only had they been deprived of the right of choice, they had been robbed of nearly $50,000 apiece—their share of the appraised value of the assets their brother and sister had taken.

Sam and Elizabeth filed a lawsuit against their siblings for return of these assets, money damages, and attorney's fees. The suit accused Bill Jr. and Dotty of fraud, deceit, collusion, conspiracy to defraud, and named their spouses as well. Bill Jr. and Dotty filed a countersuit, accusing Sam and Elizabeth of intent to defraud, collusion, unfair dealing—and naming their spouses as well. During the course of the next two acrimonious years, interrogatories were submitted and depositions taken. Temperatures ran so high that a special trustee was assigned to take over the management of the estate, and the family home and all belongings were put under lock and key. Each party involved in the lawsuit was exposed to questions about personal finances, employment history, relationship with his or her spouse, and whether they gambled or were addicted to drugs. Neighbors, employers, and friends of the parties were interviewed about them and deposed under oath, as well.

Almost three years after the filing of the lawsuits, a trial was held in probate court in Albuquerque. After two weeks of deliberation, the probate judge rendered his verdict. The court decided that the pottery in Bill Jr.'s possession was in reality the property of the state, since it had been found on federal land and was of historical value. The court ordered the items to be sent to the New Mexico Museum of Natural History in Albuquerque, and Bill Jr. was charged a $1,000 fine for each item in his possession—*plus interest* on each item, dating from the time it was taken from federal land almost fifteen years earlier. His total fine: $120,000.

The court also determined that since all four children were equally entitled under the will to receive the pottery, they were *jointly liable* for the fine.

In the matter of the artwork, a court-ordered appraisal determined it to have grown in value due to the resale of several of the paintings and photographs the DC gallery owner had purchased. Thus, Dotty was ordered to pay her siblings $25,000 apiece for the art she had taken.

Meanwhile, during a court-ordered examination of the convenience store and surrounding land, it was discovered there had been a petroleum spill on the property shortly after Bill Sr. purchased it, about which he had done nothing. And so, the New Mexico Environmental Department along with the Environmental Protection Agency ordered the property to be cleaned at the inheritors' expense and that the store be closed until approval was given by the state that the cleanup had been successfully completed. The cost of the cleanup, which was to be borne equally by the four siblings, was estimated at $150,000.

While the court's rulings could be appealed, the high courts in New Mexico (as in many other states) usually affirm the decisions of the probate judge, rendering any appeal virtually useless.

❖ Reality Check

Parental Myth: "Our grandkids will want this to remember us by."

Fact: Think carefully. When was the last time they got a phone call from the grandkids to say "hi," let alone to express fondness for a particular heirloom?

Powerful Pull

The Albright family saga defines the kind of extreme relationship collapse and financial disaster that can befall the average family over the property issue. Miscommunications and misunderstandings occur under the best of circumstances, in even the closest of families. Under the worst circumstances, such as the death of a parent and the disposition of his or her possessions, miscommunication and misunderstandings between siblings can exacerbate an already emotionally charged situation into becoming a road to hell—or to court, which in the Albright case turned out to be the same thing.

In such situations (again, the Albright case is a good example), the problem is not the property itself but the *beliefs,* the *expectations,* and the *feelings of entitlement* the respective parties have concerning that property—in other words, the emotional and other bonds they have to it and how those beliefs, expectations, and feelings of entitlement can affect and even overpower their thinking process.

That ring, watch, or necklace Mom wore, and that hammer, hat, or radio of Dad's, can exert a tremendous pull on siblings. Conversely, that same property can exert a powerful hold on Mom and Dad as well, for another important reason.

As we age, we experience a gradual loss of control over so much in our lives, ranging from our health and ability to take care of ourselves in our own homes to the ability to make simple decisions about our daily affairs. Our possessions remain a last bastion of control for us. No, we can't take them with us to wherever we go after we're gone, but we can come close—by using them to exercise our last-minute control to punish or reward those we leave behind.

This chapter, however, is not about the "why" behind our respective connections to family heirlooms or the control issues that impact our thinking about property. I'll leave that to psychologists and social scientists to address. Rather, it is about the "what" and the "who"—in other words, the disposition of that property so that the feelings of all the parties involved can be managed in a way that avoids the road to hell (or court).

The Property Conversation

The options your parents have regarding disposal of their personal property boil down to these three:

1. Make a will or create a trust for disposing of it after they're gone
2. Start giving it away now
3. Do nothing

The third choice, what I call the default position, is the natural inclination of most people. The reason for choosing it depends mostly upon whether they are parents or offspring:

• As offspring, we want to avoid conflict with those we were hatched from by forcing the issue and to avoid the even greater potential for conflict with those we were hatched with, who may not see eye to eye with us about who gets what.
• As parents, doing something—whether it's choice one or two or a combination of both—is tough physically, mentally, and emotionally, with seemingly little or no payoff other than the realization that "at least it's done!"

Therefore, the default position of doing nothing is the easier route for everybody, at least in the short run. But in the long run, it is the hardest and most painful for all concerned.

When my father became incapacitated with Alzheimer's and had to go into a nursing home, I was abruptly faced, at the worst possible time, with having to spend almost an entire week of ten-hour days going through all the possessions (not to mention papers) in his house, room by room, drawer by drawer, file by file, to inventory everything that was there, and make sure nothing was missing that was supposed to be there or that in the process I didn't toss anything one of my siblings might want. I've been exhausted in my life, but never as much as when I tackled that job. Not only was I emotionally spent from strolling down memory lane while going through all that stuff of Dad's, I suffered mental fatigue from sorting it and from the paranoia I felt as I did so, worrying about "What if I screw up?" Having the property conversation with my dad early on could have spared me all that—and would certainly have given him the "say" I know he would have preferred in his pre-Alzheimer's days as to who got what.

OK, so here's the common scenario: Your folks are getting up there and may or may not have started contemplating the idea of downsizing their lifetime accumulation of stuff and getting it under control. They have long been very clear about what they want to do with some of their property but are mostly unsure, or completely indecisive, about what to do with the rest. Here's how the property conversation might go with them.

1. Challenges

"Mom and Dad, tell me what crosses your mind when you think about having to move and what to do with all of your stuff."

Some common—in fact, the consistently *most* frequent—responses you will get include:

❖ **TIP! When to Have the Property Conversation**

My rule of thumb: have it the minute your parents give you a clue that they may be open to it. Clues can range from the frustrated cry of "I can't find anything in this mess!" to the more clearheaded and practical, "You know, your father and I have been thinking about downsizing and would like some help deciding what to keep and what to give away." The first clue is quite common; the second comes most often from parents resembling the couple that lives in Pleasantville, whose neighbors on one side are Ozzie and Harriet and on the other, Rob and Laura Petrie. But it happens. Absent any clues at all, have the conversation no later than two to three years before you anticipate your parents being unable on their own to inventory their possessions and decide what to do with things and to whom they should go.

- "We don't know how much to keep and how much to give away in terms of furniture and clothing."
- "We don't know how to divide the things we didn't want among you children."
- "We don't know what to do with what was left over."
- "We don't know how to begin."
- "We don't have the energy to sort through everything ourselves."
- "We are not able to agree what we wanted to keep and not to keep."
- "We don't know who should get Grandmother's rocking chair after we're gone."

2. Alternatives

"Mom and Dad, let's discuss some of the options that you think might be available to you in dealing with the property challenges we just discussed."

As noted earlier, the options your parents have are pretty clear, but to get them to start moving on this issue, it is important for them to actually see and express for themselves what their options are. Here are some typical examples of options parents offer:

- "Do nothing until the last minute so the decision making will be easier."
- "Decide everything now and get it over with."
- "Decide about what we can now, and put off deciding about the rest until a better time."
- "Let someone else decide for us."

❖ Reality Check

Parental Myth: "Everything can be rearranged to fit in our new home."

Fact: Perhaps—if they are "downsizing" from their current abode, not to a smaller house but to a mini-warehouse for the elderly. And for a retirement community or an assisted-living/special care facility, here's the rule of thumb about what will fit: one-third to one-half (max) of their things; some of their belongings from when they were toddlers, for nostalgia's sake, plus the addition of a Lazy-Boy—maybe.

3. RESOURCES

"Mom and Dad, let's think of some resources that you are familiar with already that we could use to help maximize your options and minimize these challenges."

Once they get going on this question, here are some typical examples that will tumble from their lips:

• "Hire an organizer to help determine how much space we have, then select the furniture and clothing we want—with the remainder of both going either into storage, to charity, to our children, or to the Dumpster."

• "Select the things we want, invite the children over to pick out what they want, and just give the rest of it away."

• "Charitable organizations from the Salvation Army to the Humane Society are always looking for donations."

• "What's the saying, 'A journey of a thousand miles begins with one step'? The first step can be to decide what to do with a single chair and then to do it."

• "Where there's a will, there's not only a way, but the energy to get there, not to mention help from others to assist us once they see us actually doing something."

• "As a couple, we haven't always agreed on everything, so when we don't agree, we just get on with it and get past it like we've always done."

• "We can leave Grandmother's rocking chair in our wills to all our children to share and share alike—and until then enjoy rocking in it ourselves."

4. EXPERIENCE

"Mom and Dad, think about the long-term care experience you would ideally like to create for yourselves as a result of the decisions you make about your property, and tell me what that experience would look like."

❖ **Reality Check**

Parental Myth: "When the time comes, we'll just have a big garage sale and get rid of everything ourselves."

Fact: By the time people reach their golden years, most have accumulated enough "stuff" to require the services of a professional liquidator to dispose of—and a young one at that. They should hire one instead to do this for them and save themselves, and you, tons of time and a severe headache.

Here are some typical responses:

• "We have all our things organized in a way that is useful for us."

• "We kept what we wanted and are no longer burdened with not knowing what to do with the rest."

• "Our place is outfitted with things of ours that are comfortable and familiar."

• "The valuables we have but aren't using and want to pass on are all safely stored away and protected, so we don't have to worry about losing them or having them stolen."

• "We were able to manage the whole process without getting exhausted, irritated, or having it turn into a big production."

• "We were able to do a little at a time over several months to let us get used to the idea and ease into it."

The Property Decision System

The property conversation will move your parents toward, at the very least, thinking about making a decision with regard to

---

❖ **TIP: It's About Making a Transition,
Not About Packing**

The property conversation is not about deciding to move to a smaller home or an institutional care facility (see chapter 6, "The House Conversation," and chapter 7, "The Professional Care Conversation"). It is about helping your parents prepare for that decision by getting leaner and meaner with their possessions *now* before a move becomes necessary. Avoid assuming that answers will come easily and that decisions will be as quick and precise as a surgical strike by a Special Forces team. Be patient. Your mom and dad will be dealing with a lifetime's accumulation of cherished keepsakes and other personal treasures, favorite tools and even appliances, plus all the memories these things will trigger as they prepare for upcoming transitions.

---

their possessions. The next step is for them to actually start making decisions. This consists of two phases: (1) taking inventory of what they have; and (2) assigning a value to each item and determining what to do with it.

I have devised a property-decision system that provides the tools necessary to complete both tasks in an efficient and organized manner, whether you will be working proactively (that is to say, with your parents in anticipation of an imminent transition) or retrospectively (after your parents are gone).

Tool number one is the Parent Care Property-Description Tool. This is used to identify each of your parents' possessions, room by room, category by category. Once the inventory is taken—whether that's three weeks from now or three months from now—the Parent Care Property-Decision Tool is used for estimating the value of each item as well as deciding and, most important, documenting what's to be done with it. For example, will they be holding onto the item or giving it away, and if the latter, to whom or where and when? The decision tool makes this task far more manageable than it may otherwise be.

The information gathered with these tools will also be tremendously helpful down the road, when it comes to settling your parents' estate. At that time, you may be called upon to provide state and local authorities with a final inventory and accounting of your parents' possessions.

Your parents have the option of using these tools on their own (many parents want to) or with your help. If they opt to go solo, however, be sure to check in with them regularly to find out how much progress they've made. If all the information has been collected and the decisions made and documented, be sure they tell you where the sheets are stored. If there has been no progress or it has become stalled, you can offer to jump in and assist. In the end, remember this: you can prod, but you can't force.

The Parent Care Property-Description Tool

Use this tool to go room by room in a systematic way, to catalog and inventory the key items you will be giving away. Granted, there will be objects in the rooms besides the ones that are intrinsically valuable, so remember, it's not necessary to go off the deep end and list everything (e.g., "blue throw rug from Target"). The idea is to create a record of your parents' possessions—what they have and/or may have had at a certain time and who has it now—so that locating and distributing those items will be an easy, straightforward task when your parents are gone. I suggest breaking the project up into mini projects by floors, so that it won't seem as daunting, and doing it as soon as your parents are close to making a change in their residence—i.e., contemplating putting the house on the market to move into a retirement community or professional care facility.

List all items

First Floor	What is stored	Where placed	Stored by whom
Foyer			
Hallway			
Living room			
Den			
Kitchen			
Great room			

Closet			
Bath			
Laundry room			

List all items

Second Floor	What is stored	Where placed	Stored by whom
Foyer			
Hallway			
Living room			

Second Floor	What is stored	Where placed	Stored by whom
Den			
Kitchen			
Great room			
Closet			
Bath			
Laundry room			
Hallway			

Second Floor	What is stored	Where placed	Stored by whom
Bedroom #1			
Bedroom #2			
Bath			
Linen closet			
Garage			
Basement			
Attic			
Other			

List all items

Personal Items	What is stored	Where placed	Stored by whom
Jewelry			
Art			
Antiques			
Watches			
Tangibles			

Assuming the property is significant and they have not made a decision about to whom it should go, this tool will assist your parents in working through that process. By asking themselves the following set of questions about each item, they will be able to determine: (a) what the property means to them and therefore what it would mean to the person they give it to; (b) who else they may want to have the item in case their first choice can't or won't

❖ TIP! Helping Parents Decide What to Do with "Stuff"

Naturally, your parents will want to keep as many of their things as possible, such as watches, jewelry, clothing, pictures, and some items of furniture, wherever they go, up to and even including an acute-nursing or special care situation. So, start with that premise and work backward, asking of each item:

1. If we stay in our current residence, would we like to keep it?
2. If we stay in our current residence, would we like to give it away now, and to whom?
3. If we stay in our current residence, would we like to store it now to give away at a later date?
4. If we move, would we like to keep it with us?
5. If we move, would we like to give it away now?
6. If we move, would we like to store it now and give it away at a later date?
7. Would we like it given away at our death, and to whom?

accept it; and (c) to avoid promising the same item to more than one person so any potential disputes will be resolved in advance.

Here's the set of questions for them to ask about each item, and how they might be answered:

• **What does this mean to me?** This pocket watch belonged to my dad and his dad before him. My dad carried it to work every day, and I remember as a child seeing it hang from a key chain around one of his belt loops. I can remember the sound of it clinking as he walked through the house. It was one of the first ways, when I was little, that I learned to recognize my dad was home from work.

· **What do I want it to mean to the person who receives it?** I have worn this watch of my dad's ever since he left it to me when he died twenty-five years ago, and every year I take it out on New Year's Day to set the time for the New Year. It is significant because it connects me to my dad. I would like my daughter to have it for the same reason, so that she can use it to remember the times that we had together.

· **Who else might enjoy this if my first choice is unwilling or unable to accept it?** If my daughter does not want to accept it, then I would like it to go to my nephew Anthony. He has always been a favorite of mine and would treasure it on my behalf the same way I treasured it on my father's behalf. I would like him to pass it on to a son or daughter of his.

· **How do I want this resolved if there is a dispute?** I don't think there will be a dispute, but if there is, I would like my daughter to have the watch no matter who is upset, as long as she wants it. If she doesn't want it, and there are two or more relatives who do, I would like their names put in a hat and the name remaining in the hat after the drawing gets to keep the watch.

· **What is my ultimate dispute-resolving wish?** My ultimate wish is that there be no dispute. But if there is one and it cannot be resolved, then I would like the watch sold and the proceeds evenly divided according to the other terms of my estate plan.

The Parent Care Property-Decision Tool

Having worked through the tough decisions on these items of personal property, use this tool to spell everything out for future reference: item, location, description, value, how the item will be distributed to the recipient, whether the recipient has been notified, and so on. In this way, there will be no doubt about what goes to whom.

Current location				
Piece of property				
Description				
Approximate value				
Prior decisions	Yes	To whom	Do they know?	How?
	Date			
Prior decisions	No	To whom		
	When?			

Averting "Nuclear Winter"

Prior to filling out a property-decision sheet for each item, parents can ask you and your siblings what you would like to take now or be assured of receiving later, and spell that out on the sheet. If nobody expresses any wants now, the property's ultimate disposition thus becomes your parents' decision all the way, and once they document it, you have to live with it.

As an added step, however, your parents can label items with the names of the people to whom they are or will be going—or even videotape themselves pointing to things as they specify, "Betsy, this, this, and this go to you when you want them," and send copies of the tape to each of the offspring or other family members. It's tough to argue about Mom and Dad's intentions with that kind of evidence.

❖ TIP! Valuating Property

Everyone's mom and dad has inherited something from their own moms and dads, or picked something up at a flea market, that Uncle Stan says will "someday be worth a fortune." If your parents, or you, suspect an item has resale value, not just sentimental value, and the suspicion is not just based on wishful thinking or Uncle Stan's analysis, have the property appraised and get its resale value established. Look under "appraisers" in the phone book for a listing of local estate appraisers. These appraisers will be able to establish not only the property's current resale value but whether that value is likely to increase and whether the item should be insured to protect its value for future recipients. The bottom line: If you think an item has resale value, get it appraised and establish that value, get it insured, and designate a recipient. If it just has sentimental value, gauge the degree of that value by who is the *most* sentimental about the item, and designate that person as the recipient.

Of course, every family seems to include at least one sibling (or spouse of a sibling) who is a staunch conspiracy theorist no matter what the evidence. My advice if you have such a sibling or spouse in the family, is to let them choose first, last, and often. Pick your battles. Unwillingness to compromise can lead to nuclear war within the family; even if you win, it will be "nuclear winter" for you the rest of your life.

❖ TIP! The Four Rules of Conflict Resolution

Unless there is clear and convincing evidence that the other party would rather rub you out than come to an agreement, assume that the person is acting in your interest on this matter, and say that it is your intention to act in a similar manner. Then follow these four guidelines for collaboration:

1. Show up ready to settle.
2. Do what is necessary to settle.
3. Never bluff.
4. Be polite.

These rules are like my Scout knife—thoroughly dependable, but if not, you will know PDQ (and so you won't waste a lot of time).

Dividing Property without Instructions

In the event your parents don't (or can't) make any property decisions, how do you divide their property with no instructions from them? Here are some possible scenarios to consider:

• Arrange a family meeting where each family member will stand up and openly state what possessions he or she wants. If such a meeting isn't possible for logistical reasons, each family member can put his or her wants in writing and send the list to whomever your parents have appointed executor of their estate.
• If two family members want the same item, these are the options: (a) assuming it's not an "I've got to have this or die try-

ing" situation, one party can opt out—yes, it does happen in some families that when two people want something but one clearly wants it more, the other will stand aside because it doesn't matter as much to them; (b) the two parties can put their names in a hat and a disinterested third party (someone not keen to have the item him or herself) can make the draw; (c) they can hire a professional mediator and abide by his or her decision; (d) they can sue each other over the item, go to court, and let all hell break loose; (e) they can share the item, if possible—for example, let's say the property is a vacation home left by your parents with no instructions to whom it should go (this happens more often than you would think), or the language of their will states that it should go "to all our children"—the interested parties can then set up a timeshare arrangement; (f) they can sell the property and divide the proceeds of the sale—a method that tends to work best with big-ticket or bulk items, such as automobiles, homes or other real estate, jewelry, furniture, and clothing.

Recognize this: when two family members really, *really* want the same item, even with the best outcome to a dispute, there are bound to be some hard feelings on the part of the one who didn't prevail. It's just human nature. Hopefully, that person will simply nurse his or her wounds, move on, and not let them fester into anything worse. To those who do prevail in any dispute, and do get to take home Dad's fishing rod, know this: at some point in your own future care situation, you will have to weigh what happens to that fishing rod next and how you want that decision to come out.

Using a Professional Mediator

If you reach the stage where you need a professional mediator, trained by or belonging to such organizations as the American Arbitration Association or the Society for Conflict Resolution, to resolve who gets Mom's needlework or Dad's high school diploma, you have reached the stage where you are about to step into a huge mess of relationship goo. Litigation is probably the final course of such action, so you might as well try a professional mediator first. In effect, he or she is the warm-up act to the "Big Litigation Show" you are about to experience if the mediation doesn't succeed.

In fact, once litigants have filed suit, our justice system will often require them to take a swing by the mediation station before going to court in the hope that a decision can be reached there. Today's swamped courtrooms, overworked judges, and aggressive attorneys pretty much assure that if every lawsuit filed were actually tried, the parties' day in court would come sometime in their grandchildren's lifetime, not theirs.

This is especially true if the property is real estate, where all sorts of factors must be considered by the court, such as the location, value, future appreciation, personal use value, legacy value, commercial versus residential zoning issues, and so on. The court will look at three likely strategies for resolving the dispute:

1. Can one party buy the other party out now or over time?
2. Can the property be sold and the proceeds divided?
3. Can the parties share in the ownership and benefits until 1 or 2 can be accomplished?

❖ DOs and DON'Ts

DO make sure you have the time to help your parents see this through.

DO encourage your parents to make these decisions now instead of later.

DO let your siblings know what is going on.

DO consult an attorney if you aren't sure what to do.

DO voice your opinion.

DO ask for help from family members.

DO document anything you take for yourself and your parents' permission to take it.

DON'T make all the decisions yourself about what should be done with the property.

DON'T treat your parents like children—it's their stuff and their life.

DON'T tell your parents what they can and cannot keep.

DON'T minimize the value of their things to them even if you're right.

DON'T ask for everyone's opinion on everything.

DON'T sell anything without your parents' approval, and document all aspects of the sale.

DON'T think for a moment you won't be criticized along the way.

DON'T second-guess yourself.

Courts as a rule are reluctant to order property sold when there are other strategies to be utilized, even if those strategies are inconvenient. There are costs to the sale, dangers of lost value due to a forced sale, tenant's rights, etc. The courts would much rather you figure this out than ask them to. Judges are, for the most part, overworked, underpaid, well-meaning civil servants who face a daily barrage of issues that would drive a wise man crazy. The last thing they want to ponder on a Friday is whether you or your brother Bob should have the house.

So, in the event of a dispute over an unassigned item of property, ask the family members who are in disagreement—or with whom you are in disagreement—if they are open to a neutral third party listening to both sides and making a decision that both parties agree to be bound by. The courts will love you for this. And you can avoid a family feud.

Resources for Organizing

National Society of Professional Organizers	www.napo.net
Professional Organizers in Canada	www.organizersincanada.com

Resources for Conflict Resolution

Academy of Family Mediators	www.mediators.org
American Bar Association Dispute Resolution Section	www.abanet.org
American Arbitration Association	www.adr.org
Association for Conflict Resolution	www.acrnet.org

6

The House Conversation

A Man's Home Is His Castle

John and Edna Williams have lived in the same neighborhood in Columbus, Ohio, for the last forty years. John retired ten years ago from Procter and Gamble as a senior vice president in marketing, and Edna retired eleven years ago as a fifth-grade teacher in the Columbus city schools. Over the past ten years, they have traveled, spent time with their grandchildren, and attended classes at the local community college, taking courses in everything from photography to bird-watching. In fact, the last ten years have been everything they dreamed retirement would be.

At seventy-five, John is beginning to slow down a bit, and Edna, while a bit more energetic, is feeling her family history of arthritis begin to take effect. Their home of forty years is a typical split-level of the kind found throughout much of Ohio, with about 3,500 square feet counting both levels. Soon after their children were born, they put in a swimming pool connected via a stone patio to the deck leading out from their family room. John occasionally swims, on really hot days, but for the most part the swimming pool is, as John puts it, "a really great place to throw money into."

❖ **Reality Check**

Parental Myth: "We can just have someone live with us. There are lots of people who are looking for room and board at a reasonable price and would be happy for the opportunity."

Fact: While there may be lots of people looking for a place to room and board at a reasonable price, I can assure you—and you in turn can assure your parents—these people are not looking for a full-time elder care job to go with it!

The house's current roof is about fifteen years old, and the guttering was replaced about twenty years ago. Here and there you can spot places on the windows that need a little work, like some caulking and paint. Generally, the brick exterior is in good condition. The kitchen, remodeled fifteen years ago, is more than adequate for their cooking needs, and maintenance, such as painting, has been reduced to the kitchen, bedroom, and bathrooms that John and Edna occupy. The other rooms are kept closed, except when their kids and grandkids come to visit. For the most part, John and Edna live in about 1,100 square feet of the 3,500-square-foot house.

Up until last year, John did most of the yard and shrubbery maintenance himself, but last fall he injured his back while spreading pine straw and fertilizer—just a silly accident that left him unable to pick up even a bale of pine straw for over six months. This past summer, he had to hire one of the neighboring boys to mow the lawn and trim. John and Edna would like to stay in their home as long as they are able since they own it free and clear, which is a great source of financial security for both of them. But John's back injury prevents him from moving between floor levels without help from his wife. Since she's not getting any younger either, they have wondered aloud to each other whether they should consider selling the place and relocating to Merrywood, a combination retirement home and assisted-living facility for people in transition, located nearby. It provides twenty-four-hour medical attention, communal and individual dining, and a recreation center for the almost daily socials and "senior connections" activities it offers.

❖ Reality Check

Parental Myth: "There's no reason for me to leave my home when I get old because I've got family and friends who have said they will stop by and check on me."

Fact: Yes, your mom or dad will be checked on—some of the time. But there won't be visitors dropping by *all* of the time. And accidents suffered by the elderly in their homes seldom occur when it's convenient for their visitors.

Edna is more open to the idea than John simply because there would be lots of new folks for her to share ideas and engage in activities with, but John complains that he would have to give up his woodworking—even though he hasn't been in his woodworking shop for over a year. (You never know, he insists, when he might want to get down to building that china cabinet he's been working on in his head for years.) This complaint, however, is just a mask for his real feelings. He loves his house even though it's getting to be too much for him, and he knows that it is. He realizes there is no way he can stay there if he suffers a major health crisis (cancer, for example), but has convinced himself that such a thing happens only to "other people." And even if it were to happen to him, he tells himself, he'd somehow figure out a way to cope. After all, he says, what's the point of having your grandkids come to visit if you can't treat them to a swim in the pool?

If you haven't yet gone through a similar experience with your own folks, or walked in John and Edna's shoes yourself, recognize this fact: *you will.*

The family home is full of shared memories; it holds a special place in the hearts and minds of our parents and in our own if it happens to be the home we grew up in. Even if it isn't a longtime residence and there is little or no generational history connected with it, it is a symbol for our parents of their self-sufficiency and continued independence, a dream we all share. It is estimated that as many as 86 percent of all Americans say they want to be able to stay in their own homes for as long as they can as they progress through their senior years, no matter how financially or physically difficult or impractical that might be. This makes it all the more difficult for any of us to suggest to loved ones like John, much less persuade them, that like it or not, for their own sake as well as the sake of others, they might have to consider moving to an assisted-living residence or nursing facility some day. It's like asking them to give up their last refuge from Father Time.

❖ Reality Check

Parental Myth: "We don't have to be in a hurry about this; when the time comes we'll know it and we'll just do what we have to."

Fact: Congratulate your folks on their unique ability to predict the future. Let's hope the future agrees with them.

It's a Woman's Castle Also

The house dilemma is not restricted to families with two aging parents. The fastest growing group of homeowners in America is single women. Statistically, women live longer than men, so it follows that most women outlive their husbands. Today, the average widow in the United States is sixty-three years old and is projected to live almost twenty years beyond the death of her spouse. While remarrying is certainly an option, statistically the odds are in the ballpark of fifty-to-one against this happening. And even if she does, the odds are statistically in her favor that she will outlive her second spouse as well. In other words, it's a better than even bet that whether she started out single as the owner of her castle or not, she will wind up that way, with all the responsibilities falling on her shoulders alone.

Mary Simpson is a perfect example. Mary is sixty-one years old. Her husband, Bob, fifteen years her elder, passed away a year ago from diabetes. She had been taking care of him for five years, seeing him through all the complications of his disease—a series of amputations, loss of vision, and eventually kidney failure. She has spent the last year recovering emotionally and financially from the ordeal.

Until Bob died, they had been living comfortably on his $4,500-per-month pension. At his death, however, the pension was cut in half. Fortunately, he had maintained a $250,000 life insurance policy, which was paid to Mary upon his death, to make up the shortfall. Their $350,000 house was owned free and clear, and Bob had amassed a $500,000 investment portfolio in the last years of his career as his salary increased. In addition, at age sixty-five, Mary will be able to collect a small $500-a-month pension of her own from her earlier working years. On the surface, it would appear from all points of view that Mary has her housing situation licked for the foreseeable future.

But let's look a little closer.

Provided she could remain in the same community, still be close to her children, and maintain her church ties, the idea of downsizing from the 4,200-square-foot, three-story home she and her late husband had shared for years is not unappealing to Mary. But she is not open to retirement-community living and is not ready for assisted living. If she were to move, a smaller home even in the 1,800- to 2,600-square-foot range will require an investment of $220,000 to $400,000, and for the most part she will be responsible herself for the yard work and other maintenance associated even with new home ownership.

Mary was diagnosed two years ago with Parkinson's disease and early-stage multiple sclerosis, facts she had kept from her late husband and her children throughout his illness. But now the mild tremors in her hands are becoming stronger and more evident, letting her know that whatever housing option she chooses, special considerations must be taken into account. For example, whether she conserves money by continuing to live in her present home or opts for the expense of a newer but smaller one, the hallways and stairways in each will have to be wheelchair-accessible to accommodate her physical needs. Kitchen cabinets, closets, and other storage facilities will have to be accessible to her from a potential sitting position, as well. Appliances offering easier accessibility will have to be purchased. In order to continue driving, she'll have to buy a new car equipped with special foot controls or specially adapted hand controls, or will have to get her current auto outfitted with them. Bathing, grooming, and showering requirements must suit her present circumstances and be made flexible enough to respond to her needs in the future in the event that her physical condition deteriorates. Mary has some big challenges facing her: all of a sudden home ownership as a single woman, even a financially comfortable one, no longer looks like such smooth sailing.

❖ Reality Check

Parental Myth: "My children have told me that they would like to buy the house from me to make sure I get the maximum value for it without having to do a lot of repairs."

Fact: Children and third-world countries share a similar philosophy about paying full price for anything. They prefer not to. And even if the children of an aging parent are willing to pay full price, they may have a financial advisor (a.k.a. their spouses) who says no.

And Mrs. M's Castle, Too

A declining birth rate, fairly steady divorce rate, and a tendency toward cohabitation in lieu of marriage has compounded the dilemma by adding extended families to this parent care issue, as well.

Consider Dan and Lois Wallace. Dan is a fifty-one-year-old Bank of America senior vice president. His wife Lois, forty-eight, works as a partner in a large local accounting firm. Together they gross about $220,000 a year, enough to pay their $2,500-a-month mortgage, $1,100-a-month car payments, $1,500-a-year private school tuition, and $10,000-a-year contribution to the college education of Dan's children from a previous marriage. Dan's mother died two years ago and his aging, widowed father is now living with them—a tense but tolerable situation. So where does this "extended family" stuff come in?

Recall the words *previous marriage* from the last paragraph? Dan was married before. His first wife died nearly ten years ago from cancer. He was very close with her mother, a widow, and has remained so ever since. In fact, he has continued helping out his ex-mother-in-law financially, even after remarrying, and his wife, Lois, has no problem with this since she gets along fabulously with "Mrs. M" (Dan's affectionate nickname for the woman). Currently capable of living alone, Mrs. M will do fine in her present housing situation, but Dan worries about her as she ages since she has no siblings and her daughter was an only child. While open to continuing to help out Mrs. M in any way they can, Lois does not see how, with Dan's elderly father already living with them, Mrs. M could come to live with them also, or how they could assist her more financially—especially since Lois's own parents aren't getting any younger either.

Now in their seventies, Lois's folks are generally in good health except for her dad's increasing forgetfulness. Hoping that it's not serious but deep down suspecting it is either dementia or Alzheimer's, she prays they can live in their home for a few more years before she has to help them consider other options. Since her mom has already declared that she will never move to a retirement home, Lois assumes that it is her responsibility to take in her mother just as Dan did his father!

Welcome to the twenty-first-century American family, where the image we once held of the traditional family unit—man and woman, first marriage, two kids and a dog, white picket fence— now represents just 12 percent of American households. The other 88 percent is made up of second and third marriages, with or without children, same-sex unions, widows, and widowers, all living in a variety of housing situations ranging from Mom and Dad in a house that's getting too big for them, Mom or Dad living alone, plus extended families from two, three, sometimes four sets of relationships and generations living alone or sharing space together. Whew! That's a lot of people with a lot of big-time choices to make about housing—and a lot of complexities to deal with in making those choices.

An Emotionally Charged Issue

Staying in one's home becomes a huge challenge when people get older, especially if a debilitating illness strikes. The majority of homes in America built before 1980 were not designed to accommodate the needs and accessories that often come with old age, such as wheelchairs or walkers. Electrical systems in older homes were not designed to handle the AC requirements of the many different pieces of medical equipment needed for today's

---

❖ Reality Check

Parental Myth: "From a psychological standpoint, it's really better for me to be in my own home than in a care facility with a lot of strangers."

Fact: Yes, I've heard the same thing said about solitary confinement. The truth is, the elderly who subscribe to this myth think they will always have the ability to come and go under their own steam, embracing the outside world or retreating from it as they please. But then they suddenly find themselves in a wheelchair, unable to leave their home without special assistance, and the place becomes a prison.

---

elderly, who are living longer lives, often in infirmity. And for seniors suffering from spells of dementia or a crippling disease like Alzheimer's, health issues combine with logistic and security concerns as well. For example, a door left unlocked at night or a wrong turn at the end of the garden could spell the difference between life and death.

In spite of all the practical reasons for doing so, engaging parents in the issue of what to do if and when their castle becomes too much for them is so emotionally overcharged it's like asking them to consider what will happen if they get divorced. Divorce is a hypothetical every married couple may be willing to acknowledge but few will want to indulge much time speculating upon.

There are so many ancillary decisions connected with the stay-or-leave strategy of the house decision, as well as so many by-product decisions that are no less stressful to make, it's no wonder families put off having the house conversation. As I wrote at the beginning of this chapter, it can be an emotional roller coaster.

So, what can you do to get your parents to sit down and face this issue with you? How can you get them to open up their feelings to you so you can develop a solution together?

The House Conversation

The CARE process is a perfect vehicle for getting into a discussion about the house issue. It gets parents thinking about a future when they are no longer living in their house but elsewhere, and to envision that future in a way that will make them feel good about it.

Keep in mind that you are not asking them to make a stay-or-move decision now, although quite often they will feel inclined to start the ball rolling after going through the house conversation with you. That is why I've included a useful house repair checklist tool and resource list at the end of this chapter for you and your parents to use when that ball starts rolling.

However, if your parents feel you are *pressing* them to make a decision now, it will typically lead to such responses as: "I'm never leaving here. They'll have to carry me out!" "I could never get this house organized enough to be able to sell it." "Who would buy this old place anyway?" And they will shut down on you emotionally, ending all hopes of a fruitful discussion for the time being.

Your objective is to get your parents to reflect on what events or other triggers would prompt them to reconsider living where they are now, and to articulate their feelings for you. For example, an offhand comment from Dad like "there seem to be a lot more steps in this house than there used to be" will tell you a lot about where his head really is on that score. The CARE process will help you smoke this out.

1. CHALLENGES

"Mom and Dad, tell me what crosses your mind when you think about continuing to live here in your own home and taking care of it or moving elsewhere if it would make life easier."

The idea here is to uncover what troubles them most deeply about the prospect of continuing to live on their own in the house as they grow older or having to move to an unfamiliar location in their golden years. The responses you get will be as varied as there are styles of houses.

Typically, what will emerge from these responses is an expression of overall panic at the prospect of losing control over some, or many, aspects of the house issue—for example, not knowing when to make a decision about the house, and perhaps making it too late, thus getting stuck with costly last-minute repairs or having to sell at a financial loss.

❖ DOs and DON'Ts

However extreme or overboard some of their concerns and anxieties may seem to you, DON'T minimize or dismiss them. To your parents, these worries are substantial and very real. Your role is to help them transform these challenges into a set of realistic possibilities for achieving a positive experience. It is up to them to minimize or dismiss what worries they may have about staying or moving by exposing those worries to the light of day and weighing them without feeling judged.

Here are some of the most commonly expressed concerns and anxieties that cause parents to put off making the house decision:

- "The house is in need of so many repairs."
- "The market is soft. We'll lose so much money if we sell!"
- "After commissions, taxes, and bank costs, we wouldn't have anything to live on if we sold."
- "Where would we go, everything is so expensive?"

The responses you get from asking the challenges question will assist you and your parents in developing a list of every fear they have about *making* a decision regarding long-term housing. Once those fears are exposed, they can be addressed.

A typical list of challenges raised by this question might look like this:

- Can't sell
- Too little money
- Too many repairs
- Bad market
- Tight credit
- Bad local borrowing
- No place to go
- Expensive future repairs
- Expensive current repairs
- Won't maximize value
- Will never see you

What do you do, now that your parents have acknowledged their fears of making a decision about staying in the house or moving out, and have spelled those fears out for you? The next step is to find out what options they see that will enable them to address these challenges and create a positive outcome.

2. ALTERNATIVES

"Mom and Dad, let's discuss some of the options that you think might be available to you in dealing with the challenges we just discussed."

The goal here is to shift the focus from apprehension over thinking about the housing issue to what your parents might gain. Some of the alternatives they come up with will surprise them. For example:

- "Sell the house and pocket the money to increase our other savings and investments."
- "Rent the house and use the extra income to supplement our new-home needs."
- "Remodel the house to allow a caregiver to occupy it jointly."

From these and other responses, you will be able to compile another list—this one of the realistic possibilities your parents have (and are now able to acknowledge) to enjoy as good and perhaps even more rewarding, a life by making a decision about the house rather than avoiding the issue.

3. RESOURCES

"Mom and Dad, let's think of some resources that you are familiar with already that we could use to help maximize your options and minimize these challenges."

By posing this question to them, your parents will begin to recognize that that they have many more resources at their disposal, both of their own and outside the family, to help them with their house decision. For example:

1. Get the house appraised to determine its true market value.
2. Have a handyman service preview the house and come up with a suggested repair list.
3. Contact a home health care agency to do an assessment of what it would take to alter the house to allow them to stay there as they age.
4. Contact a local property-management company to see what their house may rent for.
5. Contact a caregiver's association to see what the cost and requirements of a live-in caregiver would be.

4. Experience
"Mom and Dad, think about the long-term care experience you would ideally like to create for yourselves as a result of the housing decisions you will have made, and tell me what that experience would look like."

❖ Keep in Mind

Your parents' decision to leave their castle is an acknowledgment of the cycle of life. It is their statement to the world that they are entering the next phase of the human experience. Like many of life's transitions, it will bring a mixture of sadness and joy. There will be a temptation on the part of your parents (perhaps even yourself) to emphasize the former and ignore the latter—in other words, to see this transition as a conclusion that says something is over. But it is not over; it has simply become *different*.

Your parents may need some prompting here to get them going. This is, after all, a difficult question to answer even if one has been considering the prospect of leaving one's home. Contemplating leaving is a whole lot different from actually doing it. But once your folks have exposed the reasons why they feel they cannot leave (the negatives) and put them out on the table, it becomes easier to open their eyes to the positives.

Once you get started, you will be surprised at how hard it will be for your folks to stop coming up with more and more positives. This is because they will now recognize the pluses in their life and the circumstances that make facing the house decision less troubling. In turn, this will empower them to want to make a decision because they will now feel emotionally prepared to confront the issue.

Some of their responses to the experience question might go like this:

- "We no longer have to worry about the upkeep and maintenance of the grounds and the structure."
- "We are able to travel without worrying about something happening while we are gone."
- "We don't have to set aside money for maintenance and repairs."
- "We're able to increase the money we had invested in the house."
- "We don't have to worry anymore about our children disagreeing over what we do."
- "We have more time to do more things for ourselves."

From typical responses such as these, you will be able to develop a list of positives that will help spur your parents to action. I call these positives "experience accelerators," and some of them might be:

- Marketable location
- No mortgage debt
- Have maximized existing potential
- Willing to move

These accelerators, when put on paper in black-and-white, will help your parents minimize the fears they have about confronting the house issue, much less deciding it, and maximize the things that excite them about resolving that issue. They will thus be in a positive frame of mind to make a decision now—whether the actual move will be a month from now or a year from now—so that you can work together to plan for it strategically.

Think about the story of John and Edna that began this chapter; if they and their children had engaged in the house conversation using the CARE process, they would have reached a consensus together that, for the moment at least, there's no reason for John and Edna to have to pack up and find new digs right away. Other than spending a little bit of cash for pool maintenance and perhaps hiring somebody for yard work, they're fine economically, certainly for a few more years. As for John's woodworking shop, that's his vision of the ideal. With a bit more procrastination, he may avoid going in there altogether. But by keeping the workshop idea alive in his mind, he is creating a psychological hedge that provides him with hope for the future and a way to anchor his current life.

Largely because of John's personality, he and his wife Edna will very likely stay in their current dwelling longer than they should, until illness or infirmity strikes one or both of them and they have no other choice but to move to the Merrywood nursing home and assisted-living residence they've been considering. But if they had gone through the CARE process and made the decision to stay in their own home for as long as possible, they would have been able to plan for that eventuality rather than being suddenly faced with it.

❖ Keep in Mind!

Cell phone technology may be the next best thing to being there, but it isn't the same as being there, and for seniors *being there* is what counts. A sense of community is important throughout our lives but especially as we grow older. The idea of moving out of their house or apartment into a nursing home produces great anxiety in the elderly if they see it as severing the web of connections—familial, social, medical, legal—they have established over the years and disrupting their sense of community.

To Sell or Not to Sell

For many seniors, the home is their greatest source of equity and potential income in retirement. Whether they access that income through a reverse mortgage (see chapter 4, "The Money Conversation"), a line of credit, selling the home so they can afford a move to smaller, less expensive quarters, or by renting out a portion of the home for income purposes, the vast majority of seniors may have to depend upon their castle to support themselves in some way in their later years, no matter how well-fixed they may otherwise be.

Let's say the consensus is that moving elsewhere—apartment, assisted-living residence, or other type of care facility—is the best option. The obvious next question is whether to sell the house, rent it, or hold on to it. Working through this question really involves just a few straightforward considerations, after which even Hamlet would have little difficulty making up his mind:

1. Is the market favorable or unfavorable to sell?
2. How long will it take?
3. If your parents sell, how much can they get?
4. If they rent, how much can they get?
5. What is the difference between 3 and 4?

If your parents don't need the equity from a sale to live on, or rent money to get by, they may want to hold on to the home so they can come back to it if, for example, their facility stay is not permanent, or they may want to keep it for future generations. In this case, they will want to preserve that equity for as long as possible. This can be done in several ways.

One is to transfer the house into a residence heritage trust. This is an irrevocable trust that holds the real estate as a fractional or interval-ownership asset used by family members as, for example, a second home or community retreat, whereby they contribute equally to its upkeep and maintenance. Any competent attorney can set up such a trust; the trick is to provide safeguards against potential inter-sibling bickering and rivalry.

Alternatively, the house can be sold and the equity placed in a family heritage trust. This is another irrevocable trust that can be designed to survive generations. The trust principle can then be invested for growth or income (or both) to meet the needs of family members as they arise.

In the final analysis, the "stay or go" decision is really about safety. Parents may want to stay in their home but may not be safe there for a number of reasons: injuries from falls, inability to come and go, inability to follow a medicine or food regime required for their health, or a myriad of other daily financial or personal-management issues. It is important to understand that no parent except those in the most fragile physical or mental state will ever cheerfully give up their independence. At some point you must exercise that judgment for them. They will probably be angry at first, and you may feel unappreciated and perhaps overwhelmed with self-flagellating guilt for "taking their home away." If so, just remember this: your responsibility here is not to make them happy but to make them safe.

A Seller's Checklist

Most contracts for selling a house require that an inspection be made and accepted by the buyer prior to sale. To avoid surprises once a decision is made by your parents to sell their house and move, use the following tool before putting the home on the market. It is designed to help your folks get an idea of what they need to do to maximize the investment, the market value, and the equity in their home.

A member of the National Association of Realtors, a certified appraiser, or another marketing specialist in the real estate in your parents' area can then take the information you gather on this form and determine which repairs and other maintenance activities would be the most valuable to undertake to preserve or maybe even to increase the home's market value.

The Parent Care
House Repair Checklist Tool

Item	Fair	Good	Excellent	Repair	Estimate
Roof quality					
Windows					
Frames					
Sills					
Doors					
Frames					
Locks					
Body					
Walls					
Paint					
Plaster					
Wall coverings					
HVAC					
Plumbing					
Kitchen					
Bath					
Exterior					
Fencing					
Guttering					
Sprinkler system					
Appliances					
Refrigerator					

Item	Fair	Good	Excellent	Repair	Estimate
Stove					
Microwave					
Insulation					
Pavement					
Tiling					
Kitchen					
Bath					
Patio					
Pool					
Electrical					
Indoor					
Outdoor					

Resources

American Institute of Architects	1-800-242-3837 www.aiaccess.com
Contractors	Check with state boards for all projects over $500. They are required to have a license.
Handymen	The Handyman Connection www.handymanconnection.com
Interior Designers	American Society of Interior Designers (ASID) 1-800-755-2743 www.interiors.org

Remodelers	Division of National Association of Homebuilders 1-800-223-2665 www.nahb.org
Repairmen	Service Magic (www.servicemagic.com) Check out their "project estimator" help ad.

A Continuing Conversation

Older people can get along quite nicely in their homes for some period of time if they have a little extra help. That help really comes in two forms: at-home nonmedical care and at-home medical care. Sometimes the two types of care come into play simultaneously.

At-home nonmedical care includes outside and inside house maintenance and upkeep, grocery shopping, minor repair work, errands, driving assistance, laundry, dry cleaning, etc. At-home medical care can run the gamut from having someone stop by to make sure medicines have been taken to a range of treatments such as physical therapy, respiratory therapy, at-home dialysis, diabetic care, blood pressure/cholesterol checking, speech therapy, rehab work, dental care—you name it. When you consider the range of both medical and nonmedical at-home services that are available, one may ask why the transition to a care facility would be necessary at all. I address this question in the next chapter, "The Professional Care Conversation," but let me just reinforce the idea here that care facilities do play a vital role, especially in the later stages of life when more demanding care needs present themselves.

7

The Professional Care Conversation

The Care Continuum

"To stay or not to stay?" That is the question your parents will have started on the road to deciding, with your help, by the conclusion of the previous chapter, "The House Conversation." If the decision is not to stay in their current home but to move to a smaller house or apartment in the not-too-distant future, they will have begun thinking about the process of doing that as well—again with your help. The house conversation does not end here, however. It is a progressive conversation that continues with the next stage, the professional care conversation, because the question of whether "to stay or not to stay" will crop up again as the years roll by and your aging parents come to need additional and more sophisticated care and attention on a professional level.

The professional care facility experience in the United States moves along a broad continuum that looks like this:

Retirement community → Assisted living → Special care → Nursing care → Acute nursing care → Hospice → Internment

As a person moves along this continuum in the aging process, the need for professional care and services of different kinds increases accordingly. More specialists are brought in, more complex systems are encountered, and, therefore, more complicated health maintenance options must be considered. If you are having the professional care conversation, then you and your parents recognize that they are somewhere on that continuum right now. The purpose of this conversation is to learn where, so they will be able to make the facility-housing decision that is best and most appropriate for them.

❖ Reality Check

Parental Myth: "All care facilities are alike so it really doesn't matter which one I choose."

Fact: Care facilities are as different from each other as are the people who staff them and the people who live in them. I have visited so-called top-ranked professional care facilities and walked away from them with an impression of coldness and distance. I have visited Medicaid-run facilities and experienced the opposite. And vice versa. Care facilities are microcommunities with their own culture and language. It's important for parents to have a sense of whether they can connect with that culture and language.

Types of Facilities

The professional care conversation is not just about doing a building inspection. It is about the kinds of care facilities available, what each of them offers, and how they conform to the needs and expectations your parents have. For example, if your parents love art, southwestern colors, and spacious, clutter-free rooms, moving to a facility with institutionally painted walls, tile floors, and indoor/outdoor carpeting will not be all that conducive to their continued mental (and, therefore, physical) health and well-being. Conversely, in the latter stages of Alzheimer's, it's difficult for an individual to differentiate between a luxury hotel room and a closet, so the impact of their environment on their mental health and well-being will be less important. Proximity to family and simple availability of space in the facility of choice are part of the professional care equation as well.

Here is where you and your parents will get down to the nitty-gritty of spelling out the structure of care they want and will need delivered by the facility they are considering, and the level of support required to deliver that care:

• **Retirement Community.** A retirement community most resembles the traditional neighborhood or community in which your parents have probably lived, except that all the inhabitants are your parents' age or older. Modern retirement communities are much like planned unit developments where there are numerous support services, recreational opportunities, and community creation situations. Medical services, nursing staff, pharmacies, even a minihospital can be found in most modern retirement communities. While some retirement communities offer full facility integration (retirement community to nursing home), the vast majority of such communities are segmented according to lifestyle and health capabilities. Probably the most well-known national retirement community model is Del Webb Sun City, found in various cities throughout the country.

• **Assisted Living.** Assisted-living communities offer quasi-independent living within a single structure concept, with shared common areas such as dining and recreation, while allowing the residents who are able, to occupy single or double apartments within the facility. Usually round-the-clock nursing care is available with a physician on call. Mobility is usually an issue, so many assisted-living communities have a variety of planned outings and opportunities for the residents. Two well-known national assisted-living models are Brighton Gardens and Sunrise Assisted Living.

• **Special Care.** Special care is a euphemism for pre-nursing-home care. In this situation, a resident is usually afflicted with a chronic illness such as Alzheimer's disease or Parkinson's that renders the person a danger to him- or herself and others. Twenty-four-hour nursing care and staff attention are present, with either an off-site physician on call, or, at larger special care facilities, a full-time physician on staff. Special diets and meds are the norm in this type of facility. Again, Brighton Gardens and Sunrise Assisted Living are examples of facilities that offer these stand-alone capabilities, thus providing the ability to transition the resident from the assisted-living side to the special care side within the same facility as the need arises.

• **Nursing Care.** Nursing care is the choice when a senior requires the administering of specific medications and therapies of a medical nature and is unable to do this him- or herself or with the help of a family member. Nursing care may be accomplished through at-home medical care organizations, whereby visiting nurses or therapists stop by the patient's home and administer whatever is needed of a medical or therapeutic nature. Many seniors prefer to have this type of care rather than relocate to an assisted-living or special care facility. This type of care usually suggests a medical condition that is stabilized but has the potential to deteriorate and demand additional therapy that can only be provided at a facility.

• **Acute Nursing Care.** Acute nursing care is provided in facilities such as hospitals and state-run or private nursing homes because the person's mental or physical condition is in such a serious state of decline that the presence of twenty-four-hour "down the hall" medical attention is required. While there are many private acute nursing care facilities in the country that accept private-pay patients, the vast majority of such patients are dependent on Medicaid from the federal government distributed through the states.

• **Hospice.** A hospice is almost exclusively concerned with the terminally ill. The emphasis here is on acceptance of the inevitable and keeping the person as comfortable as possible. Great attention is paid to helping the individual organize his or her affairs as well as helping family members achieve closure. Many terminally ill patients may choose to remain at home until the end; hospice accommodates this choice by making at-home visits to give medicines, aid in personal hygiene, provide companionship and conversation, and even help out with the shopping.

• **Internment.** The final resting place of the individual after services or cremation. Many seniors prefer to make these arrangements themselves years in advance so as to relieve the family of this burden during a time of grief and stress.

Meet the Weinsteins

Douglas and Joann Weinstein, a couple in their early seventies, have decided to leave their family home of nearly twenty-five years and make the transition into a retirement community called Seven Springs Village, which is typical of many communities now available throughout the United States for housing our country's elderly.

They have selected Seven Springs Village because it offers, all in one location, every level of professional care they will ever need, beginning with the freedom of the retirement community experience, followed by the opportunity to transition to assisted-living apartments, a fully staffed special care unit, and then, when and if required, a hundred-bed nursing facility with acute care capabilities, located in a small corner of the development.

The Weinsteins will first be going into the independent-living section of Seven Springs Village; its housing options range from small-lot, ranch-style homes and zero-lot-line homes to quadruplex arrangements with separate porches but shared communal areas. As the Weinsteins are still able to drive, they have chosen one of the ranch-style homes with a single-car garage. In this particular section of Seven Springs Village (which, by the way, is a completely gated, secure community) they will be able to enjoy walks, a community social center, and access to an on-staff registered nurse, dietician, and physician available 24/7.

In this independent-living section, the Weinsteins will have the option of shopping for groceries at the Seven Springs food market and cooking for themselves, taking their meals (breakfast, lunch, and dinner) at the Seven Springs dining facility, or having their meals delivered via Seven Springs catering, a food service available to them at several different price levels depending on the types of meals chosen and the frequency with which they are delivered. In addition to these amenities, Seven Springs provides on-site classes on a variety of subjects, plus other educational opportunities as well as daily outings and weekly excursions for all but those who are bedridden or too infirm to participate.

All yard work and maintenance of their new quarters is attended to by Seven Springs Village staff and included in the Weinsteins' homeowner's dues. Furthermore, as homeowners, they can sell their ranch house to whomever they want, whenever they want, and move elsewhere at any time. For example, should the couple's level of independence change and their health deteriorate, they have the option of selling their ranch house and paying a monthly care fee to transition to the Seven Springs assisted-living home and receive all of the same amenities and a greater level of care. The option also exists that if one spouse can no longer live independently, but the other is able to, the latter can stay on in the ranch house while the other can move to a small apartment in the assisted-living section, and both parties can still remain in close proximity to one another.

Another very important reason that Douglas and Joann Weinstein are choosing Seven Springs is that Douglas has a family history of both Parkinson's disease and Alzheimer's. He is concerned that should he develop either of these diseases—or, God forbid, both of them—that he not be separated from Joann by having to move to another care facility. Seven Springs offers all the levels of medical care and attention Douglas will ever require, all in one locale.

Seven Springs Village is an excellent choice for the Weinsteins because it will enable them to transition from their existing home to similar surroundings without experiencing the stress of a dramatic change in environment. At the same time, they will be relieved of many of the day-to-day burdens that are becoming increasingly difficult for them to handle as they age. Seven Springs, like many other care centers being built across this country, is designed to fully accommodate the developmental path of aging seniors and to respond to their changing needs.

The Weinsteins would not have made the decision to transition to a professional care facility let alone have chosen Seven Springs Village if it hadn't been for their two children, Rachel and Adam, who had attended one of my seminars. Having observed the difficulties their aging parents were increasingly having living totally on their own, Rachel and Adam decided to initiate the professional care conversation with them. The conversation got their parents to focus on the challenges they would face in moving from their longtime home to a professional care facility from a holistic point of view, by considering the experience they would want to have as they moved along the care continuum through each phase of the transition process.

Here's how the conversation between Rachel, Adam, and their parents, Douglas and Joann Weinstein, was structured, so that you can adapt it to your situation.

1. CHALLENGES

"Mom and Dad, tell me what goes through your mind when you think about needing some form of elder care in the future."

The Weinsteins:

- "Not knowing what's available to us."
- "Not knowing how to plan for what might happen to us down the road. A facility that is good for us now may not be good for something that happens to one of us later."

• "Not being locked into a decision that we couldn't change if we needed to."

• "Keeping as much of our freedom as possible and not having to give up all our decision-making abilities."

• "Not having our money so tied up that we'd lose everything if we changed our mind."

• "Not knowing what type of care we need—or will need as we age."

• "Not being separated from each other if one of us becomes ill."

• "Not being too far away from our temple and all of our friends."

• "Not being able to leave anything to you kids because we've spent it all on housing ourselves in our dotage."

2. Alternatives

"Mom and Dad, let's discuss some of the options that you think might be available to you in dealing with the challenges we just discussed."

The Weinsteins:

• "Keep physically fit for as long as possible so we can stay put."

• "Use a service like Home Instead Senior Care to help us with grocery shopping, housekeeping, yard work, running errands, and other things that are getting to be too much for us."

• "Find a caregiver to live with us."

• "As long as you kids can stop by every now and then and check on us, that wouldn't be so bad."

• "If there comes a point when we cannot take care of ourselves or can't remember to, then we'll just trust you kids to decide what's best for us."

• "We do love seeing you and whether that's here or some-place else, we want to stay in close touch."

• "Maybe a retirement community to start with; we would want a facility that allowed us to live pretty normally unless or until we were really sick."

• "No place where there are just sick people all around, un-less we're in the same boat."

• "If we get really sick, we could go to one of those assisted-living places like your Auntie Yentl. They let her alone in her apartment except when it's time to eat, and even then she doesn't have to eat unless she wants to. They even let her keep her cat and dog as long as she can take care of them."

3. RESOURCES

"Mom and Dad, let's think of some resources that you are familiar with already that we could use to help maximize your options and minimize these challenges."

The Weinsteins:

• "If resources includes money, then we have the money to live most anywhere we choose."

• "We could do research on our own and look to you kids to help us 'surf the Net' for more information."

• "Get recommendations from friends who have already made this decision."

• "Our attorney has lots of experience helping people with these types of decisions, as does our accountant."

• "We know somebody that we can talk to who may have an ownership interest in one of those assisted-living com-munities."

4. EXPERIENCE

"Mom and Dad, think about the professional long-term care experience you would ideally like to create for yourselves as a result of the decisions you will have made, and tell me what that experience would look like."

The Weinsteins:

- "We would like to still feel as independent and in control of our lives as we do now, but without all the headaches."
- "We would want to feel safe, but not like Big Brother is keeping us under twenty-four-hour surveillance."
- "We would like to be with people who are like us, who are interested in the same things we are, and who don't define every day as either AD or BC ('after disaster' or 'before calamity')."
- "We may look and sound old and be a bit unsteady on our feet, but we still look forward to every day. So, we would want to feel that we have moved to a place where we are not just waiting to die and having the occasional visitor drop in to see if we did."
- "We love life and each other and want to be able to continue doing both even if we can't live on our own."
- "If we eventually do have to go into a special care type of place, we would still want our surroundings to be as upbeat as possible."

Choosing a Facility—the Critical Questions to Ask

Once your parents understand the level of care they need and want, use these questions to assess the list of appropriate care facilities you are helping them to consider. Give each facility a yes

---

❖ Keep in Mind!

The subject of professional care may have a multitude of meanings for your parents. It may mean the actual physical day-to-day care they will want and need—from seeing to it that they get their morning coffee and newspaper to making sure they take their daily meds to changing their soiled undies. It may also mean the emotional attention your parents want from you at this stage of their life but may not be able to articulate. In fact, the most challenging, the most sensitive, and ultimately the most rewarding part of the care conversation will be the decisions you make with your parents about the expectations they have of you and how you will be able to meet those expectations.

---

or a no for each question. When you are finished, the facility (or facilities) with the most checks in the yes column goes to the top of your list.

1. Do the buildings and the grounds create a good impression? Yes [ ] No [ ]

Here's an easy clue to look for on this one: if the building is in need of repair, the grounds are not kept up, and the grass is chronically too high, it is almost a given that the kitchen will not be in much better shape in terms of upkeep and cleanliness. It is easy to see that grass needs mowing, but not so easy to spot E coli on a countertop. Therefore, go with the law of integration: the way the outside of the facility looks is probably the way it is managed inside.

2. Is the floor plan easy to understand and follow?
Yes [ ] No [ ]

If *you* have trouble finding your way around the place, your aging parents will have a progressively tougher time of it, which can be dangerous in the event of a fire, power outage, or emergency. The physical layout of the facility should be free of complexity, making it easy to find the residence area, dining room(s), main exits, fire exits, administrative offices, and public restrooms. Listen to your own instincts: if *you* think you should be dropping breadcrumbs to find your way back from the tour, imagine the trouble your parents will have.

3. Are all the important rooms in the facility wheelchair-accessible? Yes [ ] No [ ]

Mobility is essential for residents to experience full integration into, and enjoyment of, their life in a care facility. All the rooms in the facility—not just the resident's room, dining room, and activity room—should be fully accessible by wheelchair since this will ensure accessibility to residents requiring any other type of mobility aid, such as a walker or just a cane, at any stage in their residency. If there is a platform at the front of the facility for loading and unloading wheelchair-bound residents, be sure there is an awning over it. Trying to maneuver a wheelchair-bound family member into a waiting vehicle while exposed to the elements is guaranteed to transform what is already a stressful moment for all concerned into a potentially full-fledged disaster. There should also be ample attendant staff to help assist residents with indoor and outdoor mobility.

4. Are elevators and ramps available for the physically challenged? Yes [ ] No [ ]

While Congress has mandated a number of improvements care facilities must make in this all-important area, many facilities are still playing catch-up. Make sure there are ramps throughout the facility that will enable wheelchair-bound residents access to all vital locations. Elevators should be large enough to allow a wheelchair-bound resident and an attending staff member easy maneuverability inside. Ask the director of the facility to show you the route wheelchair-bound residents must take in an emergency should the elevator system fail—or in the event of a fire, when residents are typically warned *not* to use elevators. Employ your common sense here and pretend that you are a wheelchair-bound person using the facility on a daily basis or experiencing an emergency.

❖ Reality Check

Parental Myth: "By the time I go there, it won't matter at all what the facility is like; I won't know anyway."

Fact: Nothing could be further from the truth. Elderly patients in care facilities may not remember who *you* are or why you came to see them or the names of the staff treating them or the time of day, but they respond every bit as you and I do to a kind word, a gentle touch, a hug, or other gesture of connection from you and from those treating them.

---

5. **Are all essential shelves, closets, and storage spaces easy to reach?** Yes [ ] No [ ]

A resident's physical abilities decline over time, so drawers and shelves for storing clothes, closets for hanging jackets, and so on should be within easy reach even if not used on a daily basis. Bathrooms should be roomy enough to keep soap, shampoo, toothpaste, grooming supplies, and other items easily accessible. A nightstand by the bed with a couple of drawers for various items is also a plus. While it's easy to say that things can be stored out of the way under the bed, imagine how arthritic knees and hands are going to react to retrieving those things when needed. And in memory-impaired residents, things out of reach or out of sight under a bed may as well be located in deep space.

6. Are floor surfaces skidproof and floor coverings securely fastened? Yes [ ] No [ ]

The floors of a care facility should be clean and well scrubbed, but not slick and dangerous. If a resident is allowed to bring floor coverings such as a throw rug or a carpet for his or her room, make sure the policy is that these coverings be installed with the utmost safety in mind, since this ensures every other resident must follow the same policy too. Throw rugs should be placed on nonskid matting and be free of frayed or upturned edges. Carpets should not be too thick or of a weave that might cause a shuffling resident to trip and fall. Housekeeping staff should monitor floor conditions in residents' room at all times.

Ask the management what policies and procedures are in place for preventing risk to residents in the event of hazardous situations such as spilled water or food items. A puddle of water or mashed potatoes thrown on the floor by a resident and not detected right away are, like spilled orange juice or grapes dropped in the aisle of a supermarket, accidents waiting to happen. Every facility should have portable barriers similar to the concrete barriers used on interstate highways to keep residents out while floors are being cleaned, messes eliminated, or minor maintenance completed.

7. Is there an abundance of natural and artificial lighting?
Yes [ ] No [ ]

Proper lighting throughout the facility—in common areas, residents' rooms, dining halls, hallways, dayrooms, restrooms, and so on—is an important consideration. Your parents may be entering the twilight of their lives, but that doesn't mean they should have to live in the dark. Each resident's space should have sufficient natural light available to them from a window as well as artificial light from ceilings, nightstands, and wall outlets. Wattage and color output should be appropriate to the resident's needs. Some residents are ultrasensitive to fluorescent light. Many times, bedside lamps or reading lamps are too dim or too bright, and not easily adjustable by the resident. Many female residents find it difficult to apply their makeup under fluorescent light conditions. Also, beware care centers that mimic the institutional feel of lighting at KGB headquarters or the interrogation rooms on *Law & Order*. It's a downer to visitors and residents alike.

8. Is the facility clean, fresh smelling, and free of odors?
Yes [ ] No [ ]

The way a care facility smells tells you a lot about management philosophy. All care facilities should have a policy of checking at least every hour on residents who are prone to soiling themselves. Not only is wearing a soiled garment uncomfortable to the resident, it's a health hazard and an unpleasant olfactory experience to the resident and everybody else, as well. There will always be the natural aromas of food or coffee in the air as well as the smell of cleaning agents used in keeping the facility spotless. But it's the intensity of those aromas and smells that counts. Beware of care facilities that smell like the county landfill or a Pine Sol manufacturing plant. That means something is *definitely awry.* Flowers should be present in communal rooms and allowed in residents' rooms. There should be air fresheners in every bathroom, common shower, and bathing area. Closets should be free of soiled clothing, and food should not be left on serving trays or in rooms for an extended period of time.

9. Are heating and air-conditioning units capable of handling individual usage and facility demands? Yes [ ] No [ ]

As I write this book, we are experiencing the hottest summer on record in the United States. In North Carolina, where I live, the temperature has hovered near the 100 degree mark for nearly a month. I thought I'd catch a break when I made a trip to Chicago, but the temperature was even worse there—it stood at 102 degrees! A lesser heat wave claimed nearly seven hundred lives, primarily the elderly, in 1995. Thus, it is imperative that the heating and cooling systems in residents' rooms are capable of adjusting to such extreme conditions as well as accommodating the temperature requirements of each resident. This flexibility is important because for every resident who complains the room is too cold, another resident will claim it's too hot. This is not as important a consideration in retirement communities as it is in assisted-living, special care, and nursing home situations where temperature extremes can cause accelerated dehydration. Ask the facility manager or supervisor about the capacity of the building's heating and cooling systems should demand run high in conditions of sustained extreme cold (zero degrees for a week or more) or extreme heat (100 degrees for two to three weeks). Also find out the emergency backup plan for replacement power should utility service fail. Forewarned is forearmed, as the saying goes.

10. Are handrails installed in appropriate places such as hallways and individual bath units? Yes [ ] No [ ]

I remember walking with my father in his care facility one day, when out of the clear blue his right leg gave way. Were it not for the railing along the corridor wall, he would've suffered a nasty fall. While it is impossible to imagine any care facility in our post–OSHA and ADA age not being equipped with adequate handrail and other support devices, I suspect there may still be some relics around.

There should be handrails installed throughout any special care unit and strategically placed in assisted-living units. All railings and similar support devices should be firmly fastened without any give or play.

Bathrooms for all residents should have supports enabling them to steady themselves if need be and to bear their entire weight for short periods.

11. Are there clear fire and emergency escape plans with exits clearly marked? Yes [ ] No [ ]

The disaster movie *The Towering Inferno* made an indelible mark on my young psyche when I saw it back in 1974. It impressed upon me that even the best-designed structures are subject to catastrophe under extreme circumstances, when things often don't work as planned. Always think the unthinkable about the care facility you are considering. Exits should be clearly marked, and the residents should be able understand the facility's exit strategy well enough to explain to *you* what they are to do and where they are to go in the event of a fire or natural disaster such as a tornado or windstorm. There should be enough staff on duty to assist each resident if need be in the event of an evacuation, as well. Never just assume that management has thought about these things and has a plan in place. Ask for specifics.

12. Is the facility financially solvent? Yes [ ] No [ ]

While most facilities will be reluctant to let you look through their income statements and balance sheets, if you ask they will usually reveal how many months of operating cash reserves they have on hand in the event of emergencies. The local Better Business Bureau is another source for determining how solvent a facility is because there you can find out if it has been the subject of any fiscal complaints or litigation. Also check any records of lis pendens ("suit pending") in the files of your local courthouse to see if the facility is subject to creditor claims or actions. You can also use your own eyes as a resource to gauge how flush a facility is just by eyeballing how cash is being spent in the place. If the facility appears to be understaffed given the number of residents, if the furniture and fixtures are unduly worn and the supply closet bare, you can guess pretty accurately that the facility is operating on a tight budget.

A less traditional method of getting a fix on the money situation is to ask management what the facility's "rolling resident occupancy rate" is. Residents, you see, are a source of cash flow; just as in a motel or hotel, the ability to provide services is dependent on occupancy and room rate. The higher the occupancy and room rate, the more services will be available.

My *favorite* nontraditional method of monitoring a facility's cash flow status, however, is to pop in at a mealtimes and see what's being served. The fresher the vegetables, the greater the variety of protein sources, and the more natural the starches and carbohydrates, the better the facility's cash flow and overall solvency probably are. Here are a few clues: no matter how well-cooked, broccoli is never beige; there are more parts to chickens than just wings; and a slice of ham is not translucent if held up to the light.

13. Is the facility adequately staffed and in good standing with regulatory agencies? Yes [ ] No [ ]

Without sufficient support staff at the facility, you will find yourself making countless trips to the emergency room at the hospital to retrieve your parent after treatment for problems of as little seriousness as an attack of gas! All states have guidelines as to the appropriate number of staff per resident a facility is required to maintain. Like the FDA's recommended daily allowance for vitamins, however, these are *minimum* standards.

Each facility should have enough staff members to ensure the following: (1) if a staff member fails to report for duty, a substitute can be found and on the job before that staff member's shift is over; (2) there is enough staff to ensure that baths, daily cleanings, and resident meals are served on time and without unnecessary delay; (3) that all medicines are dispensed with the frequency and in the dosage expected per documentation.

Furthermore, there is absolutely no excuse today for inadequate background checks on all current personnel and those applying for future openings. The Internet allows even the oldest of care facilities to easily ascertain information—from past pedophiliac acts by individuals, to prom dates—on almost any individual.

14. Is there a registered dietician or nutrition expert on staff? Yes [ ] No [ ]

Whether it's a retirement or assisted-living community, special care unit or nursing home, expert nutrition and meal advice is critical to the health and well-being of residents. The elderly often find themselves caught in a "perfect storm" of nutritional conundrums:

***

❖ TIP! Interacting with Staff

I have seen the offspring of the elderly in assisted-living, special care, and acute care facilities treat staff members as if they didn't exist or as if they were their parents' personal servants. These staff members are typically underpaid, overworked, and often completely unappreciated for the services they perform. As someone who has helped serve meals and clean up the dining room on weekends along with staff throughout my father's five-year stay at a care facility (I still help out at this facility on weekends), I know for a fact that most of the folks working there are angels in disguise. Most people are not up to the task of doing for one day what these folks do every day. So, unless you see a staff member commit a terrible infraction, ease up.

***

little or no appetite to begin with, plus mandatory medicines that kill appetite, plus declining physical abilities that limit exercise and decrease appetite. These combinations are recipes for disaster. A registered dietician or nutrition expert on staff at the facility will make sure that your parents are eating enough, eating the right things, and eating responsibly in relation to their current physical state and medical protocols—for example, that diabetics do not have free-range access to the dessert bar and that Alzheimer's patients aren't allowed to eat like lumberjacks when they can't remember when they last ate (which was twenty minutes ago).

15. Does the facility maintain an in-house nurse or available physician on call 24/7? Yes [ ] No [ ]

Granted, having nurses and physicians always on call is expensive, probably the most expensive line item in a care facility's budget. But they are a must. Ideally, there should be a registered nurse or physician on staff 24/7 at acute care facilities. If not, find out what the response time is for the nurse or physician the facility has on call 24/7. With today's cell phones, pagers, and Blackberries, response time should be close to immediate. But if the response is a recording that says, "You have reached the medical offices of Doctors We Don't Give a Flip, please leave a message and we'll get back to you as soon as we can during normal office hours," look for another facility.

❖ TIP! Emergency Services Policy

Most care facilities have access to emergency medical personnel through the 911 system or speed dial to the emergency room at the local hospital. If the hospital is Boston General, the process is going to be a little more complicated than if it's Mayberry General and Aunt Bee who answers the phone there. The local fire and police departments are often staffed with EMTs as well, who can perform on-site diagnostics or at least transmit vitals to people who can diagnose. The larger consideration is the facility's policy for using emergency services. In a health care environment shell-shocked by an onslaught of malpractice litigation, a knee-jerk response policy is more often the rule than the exception. A severe headache demands less acute treatment than a heart attack, but they both require a reasonable response policy. Emergency transport and treatment are expensive. But in the end it is better to err on the side of caution and send someone to the ER unnecessarily a couple of times than to not send him or her there the one time it is critical to do so.

16. Is the nearest acute care facility or trauma center close enough to provide fast response? Yes [ ] No [ ]

Most populous areas in the United States offer relatively fast access to an acute care or trauma hospital by highway or air ambulance. A good rule of thumb is for the care facility you choose to be no more than thirty minutes to an hour away from a trauma center and to have excellent transport capabilities (an ambulance equipped with state-of-the-art technology and not Bob the nightman's Explorer with seats folded down to spread Dad out on an army blanket). Response time will vary from location to location depending upon availability and weather conditions. Conversely, if the local EMT response time is always "We'll get back to you after dinner and see what we can do," consider a care facility with better capabilities and trauma center connections.

17. Does the facility offer a written plan of care and have the flexibility to adapt it to the residents' changing needs? Yes [ ] No [ ]

A written care plan is important for several reasons. First, it spells out the type of care provided to elderly residents so that you, the layperson, can get a pretty good idea of what your parents can expect to receive. Second, a written care plan will usually stipulate that you are allowed to meet the staff or the managers supervising the staff who will be providing that care so you can ask questions. This written plan is what I call the "parent operating system" (POS) for your folks while under the facility's care. Make sure to go over it with your parents carefully. And take the initiative to get updates so that you will know if the POS has been modified. A sudden change in your parents' physical or mental state as a result of such a modification could prompt a change in their medical condition that will need to be addressed in a change of medical protocol. Do not just assume that everything is happening according to plan or that if a change occurs, or is required, the facility has the ability to flex and is right on top of things.

The Ten Warning Signs of Negligence and Neglect

In a care facility where there are dozens, sometimes hundreds, of patients all suffering from various complaints, ailments, and illnesses to different degrees, one cannot expect a perfect record of care all the time. Why not? Environment is one reason—it's a care facility, not the Four Seasons. Staffing is another reason. Care facilities are staffed by wonderful, dedicated people with the best of intentions. But overcrowding, overwork, and stress take a toll. Expect the ball to get dropped from time to time. But there is a vast difference between your dad not having his pitcher filled with fresh water one day and his being medivacked to a trauma center due to acute dehydration. Look at trend lines. One day without a bath could mean your mom slept late, didn't want a bath, or was too difficult to handle that day. An entire week without a bath means someone isn't doing their job.

WARNING SIGN 1: *Your parent's personal hygiene is not being attended to on a daily basis.*

Oily hair, food particles in the teeth, and body odor are sure signs that bath time and brush time are being neglected. Pay particular attention to toenails and fingernails, as they are more disease-friendly than almost any other part of the human body. Toenails, especially in diabetics, can be a source of infection and disease if not trimmed properly.

WARNING SIGN 2: *Your parent is noticably losing weight.*

This could be a function of a number of things: not eating, not taking in enough calories, improper diet, onset of diabetes, depression, or undetected cancer. Any weight loss noticeable enough to get your attention should be getting the staff's attention first.

WARNING SIGN 3: *Your parent is always asleep, listless, or unaware of your presence when you visit.*

These symptoms could be signs of a deteriorating physical condition, excess or inappropriate medicines, depression, lack of exercise, or perhaps even an unbearable roommate. It's normal for the elderly to have good days and bad days—and more of the latter the older they get. But unless your mom or dad is in the final stages of a chronic, fatal illness, it's not normal for them to be having a bad day every time you visit.

WARNING SIGN 4: *Your parent complains of mistreatment by staff.*

Granted, older people complain more than young people (except for seventh-grade girls, who complain all the time in my experience as a dad), but even older people are not inclined to complain constantly *unless there's a reason.* Sure, they will create mountains out of molehills just to get attention or spawn tales of mistreatment and how "awful this place is" simply because they suddenly may not want to be there. But don't assume this is the case. *Investigate* all *complaints of mistreatment!* Somewhere between "the food here stinks" and "Nurse Betty came at me in the shower with a knife," there may be an element of truth worth pursuing.

WARNING SIGN 5: *Your parent has unexplained, frequent, and unusual bruising or pressure marks on the body.*

Nursing home abuse and neglect are staple fodder for newspapers, periodicals, and made-for-TV movies. And the reason why, is that such abuse occurs—more frequently than we would like to believe. Imagine being in a room with your elderly father or mother bitching about everything to the tenth power. Multiply that by the number of other residents in the facility, all of them bitching about everything to the tenth power as well—all day, every day. Some environments are just conducive to abuse. But that's no excuse for it.

WARNING SIGN 6: *Your parent's personal belongings keep vanishing.*

Disappearing socks or underwear, a missing wristwatch, a vanished ball cap can be the result of several things: your parent's laundry got mixed up with that of another resident; your

---

❖ TIP! Keeping Tabs

Presumably, you wouldn't leave a toddler off at day care and not check back for weeks at a time to see if he or she were safe and healthy. Well, the same goes for your parents at a care facility. The best way to make sure they are being well taken care of is to see and talk to them frequently—and to regularly check on the care facility's treatment protocol to see that their program of care is being adhered to. If you cannot physically visit your parents often, then call them at least weekly and follow up with a telephone call to the staff member in charge of administering your parent's care. There is no excuse for not staying in touch with your parents at their care facility and keeping up on their physical and mental well-being, no matter how far away it is from you.

parent left it in a room he or she was visiting but can't remember which room; it was stolen by another resident; someone visiting your parent's roommate picked it up and put it away thinking it was the roommate's; some of the facility's staff members have light fingers. The way to prevent all this from happening is to print your parent's name on each item he or she takes to the facility or adds while living there. Keep an inventory of these items and run a periodic check to make sure all are present and accounted for. If not, check with the laundry service to see if it has the socks or underwear that disappeared. Keep an eye peeled for a resident wearing your dad's missing shirt or a staff member with his vanished Seiko.

WARNING SIGN 7: *Your parent keeps going AWOL.*

Most care facilities are required to log a resident out and in again when he or she goes off premises and returns. Unauthorized departures must be logged, as well. No matter how good the care experience may be, at some point most residents, especially of nursing homes, will come to view the place as more of a prison than a refuge because they're unhappy, scared, bored, or abused (or think they are). Thus, a door left open becomes an invitation to, and an avenue of, escape. In the early days of my father's stay with Alzheimer's, he was aware enough to know that he didn't want to be where he was but not aware enough to remember why. He would loiter in the hallway by the exit doors to the special care unit, and when someone went in or out, he would use his cane to hold the doors open so he could slip away. If your parent keeps trying to "escape" (and is succeeding!), confront the staff right away as to how and why.

WARNING SIGN 8: *There are increasing unexplained medical and maintenance costs.*

All medical procedures and costs should be itemized for you by the care facility on a separate bill or included as part of your overall statement. Be sure to ask during the initial interview what past increases for basic services have been and what the facility anticipates rate increases to be in the future. Many facilities charge a premium for special care sections for patients with Alzheimer's or Parkinson's disease and other debilitating diseases. Also, in some cases, an expensive drug may be prescribed with the best of intentions but will prove to have little staying power, or may not work at all, yet routinely continue to be prescribed—and routinely you continue to pay the cost. In my father's situation, for example, he was given a prescription for a costly memory-improvement drug that in the end seemed to have no effect at all. Review any drug recommendations in consultation with your parent's physician.

WARNING SIGN 9: *Your parent's skin is overly dry and cracking.*
There may be a number of explanations for this: dehydration, the temperature in the facility is kept too hot, the air is too dry and the resident needs a humidifier, lotions or creams are not being applied to your parent's skin to ease the problem. A good care facility will have a dermatologist available for consultation in the event you and/or staff notice undue dryness on your parent's hands, elbow joints, or around their eyes. Keeping skin lubricated is often overlooked in older residents, but dry, flaky skin can be the breeding ground for nasty infections.

WARNING SIGN 10: *Your parent complains of chafing or rash in the buttock area, or you observe the presence of small ulcers on the back and legs.*
Bedsores are not a medieval phenomenon. They occur almost routinely in the elderly population, especially those who

are bedridden for extended periods. Most facilities will have a protocol for making sure that immobile or bedridden residents are shifted frequently so that pressure sores or ulcers do not develop. Rashes and irritations often appear around the buttock and groin area on both men and women due to incontinence and sitting in soiled undergarments for extended periods. Candidly, in any modern care facility there is no justification for the presence of bedsores or the irritations described. If you see your parent developing them, confront the nursing supervisor or the facility's director of physical therapy *immediately.*

❖ TIP! It's Not Just About Holidays and Birthdays

Typically, when they reach the point where professional care is required, what the elderly need most to sustain them are the three *c*'s: connection, community, and conversation, especially with the children whom they brought into this world. Statistically, the average stay in an extended care facility is between four and six years. Step up your visitation schedule to include more than just birthdays and holidays.

National Resources for Locating a Professional Care Facility

Home Instead Senior Care	www.homeinstead.com
Retirement Living Information Center	www.retirementliving.com
	203-938-0417
Senior Resource	www.seniorresource.com
	877-793-7901

American Association of Homes and
    Services for the Aging

www.aahsa.org
202-783-2242
202-783-2243

Adult 55+ Communities

www.activeadulthousing.com
877-55-ACTIVE

Covenant Retirement Communities

www.covenantretirement.com
800-255-8989

WEBB Active Adult Communities

www.delwebb.com
800-808-8088

8

The Legacy Conversation

What Is a Legacy?

Legacy is about remembering the past in order to make sense of it. Remembering is also about bringing organization to the present so that it transcends the past, and designing a future that integrates all that has gone before, in honor of that past.

History, some might say, is essentially an exercise in revisionism, while legacy falls more into the category of reconstruction: it is a way of identifying and celebrating the progress we have made over the course of our lives. And I guarantee there is not a soul, living or dead, who failed to make some manner of progress during his or her time here on the planet. Being born is by itself a milestone step on the progress path; think of it, 50 million sperm all after one egg—and yours won out! Learning to speak, to walk, to write, to learn, and to relate, to provide for

---

❖ Reality Check

Parental Myth: "When I'm gone, I'm gone. I don't care if future generations remember me."

Fact: Of course not. That's why you've got all those albums full of photos dating back to your first-grade graduation and that huge record collection and every cup from Dairy Queen you ever had a date-night sundae in stashed around the house that you say should go to this person and to that person when you're gone. You've kept these things because they're like stored memories of the events, the interests, and the passions that symbolize you. The simple truth here is that parents who make this statement are usually those who want to remember and be remembered the most. My dad said something very much like it in his last years. After I responded, "I know you don't care, but if you did, what would you want everybody to remember?" He talked nonstop for the next hour.

---

oneself and others—all are huge milestones in our personal progress along life's path.

Our legacy is, perhaps, the last step on that path, a summing-up of our life's journey along that path and what that journey has meant to ourselves, as well as what we want it to mean to those who will follow and may even be able to benefit from our having "been here."

Shattered Legacy

Russell Simpson was the owner of Simpson Products ("Simpson Box" the locals called it), a corrugated container manufacturing company in Austin, Texas. Through his company and on his own, Russell was a big supporter of many local charities as well as the local Methodist church where he and his wife, Ilene, and their three children (two sons and a daughter, all of whom have worked in the family business since graduating from college) attended services every Sunday.

With retirement age looming, Russell Simpson went for his annual physical and was told by his doctor that he had developed an incurable form of cancer; his prognosis gave him about a year. Accepting his fate with the dignity and grace of a man who has lived fully, completely, and is comfortable with his future in the hereafter no matter what form it takes, he immediately went about the business of getting his affairs in order.

He made numerous attempts to talk, one-on-one and collectively, with his three children about what he wanted to happen with the company, the gifts he wanted to make to each of them, and his dream of funding a new wing for the Methodist church that would serve as a combination gym and classroom facility for the kids in the community. But his children were unable to face, let alone talk with, him so openly about his impending demise. On each occasion that he attempted to sit them down for such a discussion, they would either find an excuse to change the subject or reschedule the meeting ahead of time.

Russell went ahead and met with his pastor at the church to discuss his plans for the new wing; based on those discussions, and Russell's assurance that he had the financial wherewithal to bankroll the project, the pastor urged the church board to request proposals from contractors right away in the hope that the new gym and classroom center might be completed in time for Russell to attend the opening ceremonies.

Russell also visited several other organizations—the Salvation Army, the Humane Society, the Children's Care Center—to inform them of the donations he would be making to them through his estate, and they too set about making plans accordingly.

Meanwhile, Russell's children remained in complete denial of his condition and all the issues relating to that decision that swirled about them. It was all too painful for them. But then, events took an even more painful and tragic turn.

Two months before Russell was to enter the hospital for his final stages of care, he and his wife Ilene were killed in a freak two-car collision outside of Austin. The loss of their father and their mother at the same time totally devastated the children.

At his death, Russell had yet to finalize his complex estate plan and sign all the required documents. There turned out to be insufficient liquidity in his estate to pay the tax obligations due the government, so the children were forced to bring in a venture-capital partner to raise money to keep Simpson Products in operation and pay the estate taxes. The new partner immediately called a halt to any future donations by the company and refused to honor the financial commitments Russell Simpson had made to the Methodist church and other charitable organizations. Unfortunately, the Methodist church had committed itself financially to building the new wing and the failure of Simpson Products (and thus the Simpson family) to deliver on Russell's promise put severe stress on the church's budget and cast Russell's memory in a bad light among its board and parishioners. Instead of a monument to Russell Simpson and his philanthropy, the new wing had become a financial albatross around the church's neck, and the good name of Simpson Products was declining rapidly, not just with the church but with the other organizations to which Russell had promised contributions, as well.

Within two years of the deaths of Russell and Ilene Simpson, the venture-capital partner the Simpson children had brought in to save the company merged "Simpson Box" into a larger operation in San Antonio and bought them out. Many employees who had been with the company for years elected not to transfer to the new location for various reasons and thus had to take an early retirement or resign.

Russell Simpson's lifetime of work, commitment, and industry was gone overnight. Surely, this was not the legacy he had in mind for himself, his wife, or his family.

The loss of the Simpson family business, a community company and generous contributor over the years to many community causes, might have been prevented if rather than evading the reality of their father's mortality, the Simpson children had forced themselves instead to sit down with him as he had wanted, to address his legacy concerns, goals, and desires. That is what having the legacy conversation is all about.

❖ Reality Check

Parental Myth: "I can take care of managing my own legacy without any help."

Fact: Yes, and the paint-by-numbers industry makes a small fortune out of convincing people they can be artists. Remember how the legacy of Russell Simpson got totaled—and he didn't start out thinking or even wanting to manage his legacy on his own!

As a result of having the legacy conversation, you and your parents will come to understand, and thus be able to act on, their legacy wishes as regards:

• **How your parents view *themselves* and their lives.** Except, maybe, for serial killers, most people want at some point to gain some perspective on their lives. As human beings, we have a deep need to build connections and to establish transitions for ourselves as a way of gaining perspective on how we have lived and what we have achieved along the way. Discussing legacy concerns with your parents builds a connection and establishes a transition that allows a legacy strategy to be designed. Parents who were teachers obviously spent a great deal of their lives in pursuit of knowledge and sharing that knowledge with others. A scholarship in their name for a child—whether awarded based on need, achievement, or random drawing—acknowledges their commitment in a tangible way. Similarly, parents who loved and cared for animals all their lives can continue their good work with a gift in their name to the local Humane Society or animal shelter.

• **How your parents want *you* to remember them.** The process of raising children involves making them do things we don't particularly enjoy making them do (and that they often don't like or want to do). This is all part of the experience of transforming children from wild animals into (hopefully) responsible, contributing adults. Inevitably, though, the tensions that arise from this experience will impact the parents' and the child's respective memories of those key child-rearing/growing-up years. As a result, after the parent is gone and the child reflects on those years, he or she may remember the parent a different way than the parent would like. For example, most parents would hope that their kids remember them more for their persistence, courage, and loyalty in supporting the family than for the numerous times they grounded the kids as teenagers for smarting off at them. The legacy conversation is a way of setting the record straight about the lifelong parent–child relationship and gaining some lasting perspective on that relationship so that, for example, parents can *know* their children will always remember them not as the prison guards they on occasion had to be but as the human beings they are—and always were.

• **How and by whom your parents also want to be remembered.** All but the most reclusive and isolationist among us accumulate friends over the years, and are, thus, part of a larger community—be it a church, synagogue, Rotary Club, or YMCA. These associations produce relationships that also create memories. Whether it's with a generational family portrait, plaque, award, donation in their name, or whatever, parents may wish to be remembered for the part of their life they shared with those folks and organizations, too.

• **What your parents want others to remember them for.** I remember watching Senator Edward Kennedy's eulogy on behalf of his assassinated brother Bobby on television back in 1968. While undoubtedly there were hundreds of ways the senator could have memorialized his slain brother, he did so simply, and powerfully, as a "good and decent man." He then went on to explain what he meant, concluding with the message that his brother "saw war and tried to stop it." I still think of Bobby Kennedy that way. Our parents too want to be remembered not only for who they were and what they achieved in life, but for the many worthwhile things, large and small, they sought to achieve for others and that gave their lives meaning.

The Legacy Conversation

The overall aim of the legacy conversation is not to come up with a checklist of pros and cons about your parent's life as a way of scoring whether that life was well spent or not. It is to continue the process of empowering them to feel the confidence they have built up from the previous conversations and to carry it through to this final parent care issue as well. Your role here is to focus your parents toward thinking about their past and to get them to communicate their thoughts and reflections to you from the perspective of the present, so that together you can start ensuring that legacy by taking strategic action.

Here's how it goes.

1. CHALLENGES

"Mom and Dad, think about how you would like to be remembered and tell me what goes through your mind."

What you are trying to get at here is your parents' view of their history and the struggles they faced, individually and as a couple, while making their way in life. They had bills to pay, children to feed, and jobs to consume their time and attention. There must have been periods when they were feeling on top of the world and periods when they thought they would never get off the bottom. Each situation served to create the people they became and, thus, how they wish to be remembered.

Typically, as parents begin to open up on this, they will share some, if not all, of the following. For some of you, it will not be the first time you have heard many of these things. But it may be the first time you actually *hear* them, and the experience can be an eye-opener. Tales you might hear include:

- The story of their humble or ostentatious origins and how they triumphed over one or the other.
- The story of their first job and the career path they chose (or that chose them) and led to where they are now.
- The story of meeting their mate (your mother or father), falling in love, and creating the family of which you are a part.
- Their moments of joy and heartache from both the work involved and the excitement they experienced in raising a family.
- Stories of the places they lived or visited, and the memories they have of those places.
- Stories about the friends they made growing up and into adulthood.
- Stories of relatives you may not know or remember, who were funny, interesting, or just plain weird characters that contributed to your parents' life experience.
- Favorite anecdotes, favorite times, and specific events they treasure and remember most.

2. ALTERNATIVES

"Mom and Dad, let's discuss some of the options that you think might be available to you in dealing with the challenges we just discussed."

During the course of our lives, we all make decisions we wish we could take back or wish we had made in a different way. These missed opportunities and what we learn from them define us as well. But this question is not about brooding over past regrets; it's about helping your parents focus on and appreciate (perhaps even relish) what was—the things they did well and wouldn't change, which benefited themselves and others

> ### ❖ Reality Check
>
> **Parental Myth:** "I'm no storyteller. Besides, I have no great stories worth telling."
>
> **Fact:** Raising children, housebreaking a puppy, planting roses, painting a barn, the first car, the first date, the first grandchild—all are fodder for stories that come out of our lives and the laughs we experience recalling them. My father must have told the story about the longest train he'd ever seen nearly 5 million times in his life, but the last time he told it, I heard something different, something I'd never thought of before. Now that he is gone, I can still hear him telling that story, and the memory of it is a great thing.

because they made those choices—and not "might-have-beens" that will bathe them in remorse. From conducting thousands of hours of these conversations, I can tell you this: If you think of the course of your life as the hours from noon to midnight, the things most people would change or do differently in their life if they could would take up the last five minutes, from 11:55 to midnight, to accomplish. The number of "might-have-beens" is barely worth considering, let alone regretting.

In many ways, this conversation will enable your parents to shed any regrets they may still have, by acknowledging the important lessons they have come to understand from the decisions they made (which were right for them at the time), and which can be passed on.

Some typical alternatives that will come up in response to this question are:

- "We would've started a savings and investment plan sooner."
- "We would've taken more vacations to interesting places."
- "We would've not worried so much about things that didn't really matter."
- "We would've spent more time at home and less time at the office."
- "We would've spent more time with you children."
- "We would've been kinder and more considerate of each other."
- "We would've made more friends."
- "We would've worked through our problems rather than giving them short shrift or running away from them."
- "We would've had careers rather than just jobs."

3. RESOURCES

"Mom and Dad, let's think of some resources that you are familiar with already that we could use to help maximize your options and minimize these challenges."

This question allows your parents to toot their own horn a bit as well as to recognize the contributions to their lives others have made along the way. Face it, none of us would be able to make it in life without the help, the inspiration, and what we learn from others—even if "others" means those puppies, the guppies, and the hamsters on wheels we grew up with that played a big part in our formative years.

Here are some of the resources parents have said they drew upon in life:

- Books and learning
- Travel
- Different jobs

- Relationships
- Births
- Deaths
- Friendships
- Spirituality and faith
- Financial skills
- Tenacity
- Foresight
- Integrity

Just look at that list. It tells you a lot about those people, doesn't it—as parents *and* as human beings!

4. EXPERIENCE

"Mom and Dad, if you were to describe the legacy you would like to create as a result of all the long-term care planning decisions you have made, what might it look like?"

What you're trying to achieve with this question is to get your parents to see their life as an *experience*—and what they want others to take from that experience about them. You may have to do some prompting here to help them to reflect on their lives from that perspective, which will involve overcoming any tendency they may have toward false or excessive modesty. It is not prideful to want to be recognized and remembered for the good you did in your time on earth *just being you.* I'm sure that while we can all admire and respect the symbolic remembrance and anonymous recognition offered by the Tomb of the Unknown Soldier, few of us would wish to be buried there.

You want your parents to see that while they were finding their own way in life, they were also finding the way for, and even guiding, others—like yourself.

Their responses might go something like this.

"We always did try to help those less fortunate than ourselves and to show a strong work ethic to you kids because we
feel a job worth doing is worth doing well. And so we never
gave up on anything or anyone. If we can have some recognition for that, well, it's only human nature to want to have it—
for us, for our children, and for the generations to come."

❖ TIP! Ways of Remembering

Here is a sample of the ways your parents can be
remembered tangibly for their life experience. Expand on
this list by involving your parents in coming up with their
own ways of symbolizing their memory—then work on
making it happen:

1. A room, wing, chapel, etc. in a local hospital
2. An annual fund-raising event such as a walk, bike
   ride, or bake sale
3. A festival, gathering, production, or some other type
   of artsy event
4. A matching-donor pledge program up to a certain
   amount

My Story, Redux

It was one of those fall days in the South that is remarkable for
its clarity and its color; evening had come, yet the air was still
without a trace of humidity.

My dad and I were sitting in rocking chairs on the porch of
his care center. It was early on in his bout with Alzheimer's, before the disease had erased his memory of the past, his aware-

ness of the present, and his ability to contemplate the future. At that moment, he was aware— he was "back" as they say about Alzheimer patients—no, not exactly back like he used to be but clearly back enough to have a conversation. You see, it is one of the cruel ironies of Alzheimer's that on occasion the brain rights itself, and for brief periods—hours sometimes but mostly moments—the afflicted resembles his or her old self before the identity-destroying disease grabbed hold.

The whole idea of a Parent Care Solution program and its accompanying parent care conversation methodology was still in the incubation stage. But since he was back and aware, I decided to raise the legacy issue, though I didn't call it that at the time. I asked him how he would like to be remembered. After what seemed like an eternity, he responded: "I would like people to say that I was honest, that I cared for my family, and that I always tried to do what was right. Oh, and another thing— that you could always depend on me."

I asked him which of those he would like to be remembered for most. He replied without hesitation, "That I took care of my family."

I asked him if he had any concerns about being remembered that way, and he said there were times when he had to be tough on us kids when we were growing up, and that he worried we'd remember him mostly from those times, as just this tough, hard guy instead of as a guy who was only tough and hard when he had to be because he believed it was necessary. He was really more than that.

I told him that I thought he had created a remarkable life for himself and our family, and that the very hard, poverty-stricken West Virginia background in which he'd been raised may have been not just the origin of his toughness but the inspiration for him to do well by himself and all of us. That opened the door, and for the next hour he talked and talked about how growing up really poor had helped him to appreciate every little thing. About how he had learned to ride a bicycle without using his hands so that he could keep them warm in his pockets on bitter cold days ("I could ride five miles or more like that," he said). About the war—I mean the big one, World War II—where he'd been a sailor on the USS *North Carolina* during the brutal battle for Peleliu, the Japanese front line of defense in the South Pacific, and how witnessing all the wounded and the dying brought on board from the bloody shoreline had made him feel sick to his stomach and like dying too. The war was one of the most horrible things he had ever experienced, he told me; it had changed him forever. Only the thought of his family back home kept him going, he said.

Dad paused for a second, flashing back to his childhood again, and shared a thought about growing up on a farm—how it had given him his respect for hard work and the value of doing a day's work for a day's pay. *Earning* his money throughout his life was a real source of pride to him. He then told me about getting the same toy wagon two years in a row at Christmas. The first year it had been brand new. The second year, his parents could only repaint it for him to look like it was new because the Depression had hit and times were hard.

As I listened, it occurred to me that it is in the remembering of the stories of our lives that we live forever. "I am what survives me," the philosopher Erickson wrote. Our stories are what survive us.

My dad and I were never able to talk like that again. Over the next few months, then years, the disease that had so insidiously entered his life took that life over, and our get-togethers dwindled to exchanges of smiles and the simple "Hi, how are you?"

type of greeting that Alzheimer's makes inevitable. But that late-coming and fragmented legacy conversation had helped to bring a sense of closure—to both of us, I believe, but to me certainly. It allowed for a different kind of communication, one that connected us in a way we had never been connected before. Most important, it resulted in the telling of his story—in random bits and pieces, maybe, but those pieces will remain in the hearts and minds of my family and myself, and will continue to be told around the Taylor family campfire for generations to come.

Five years after that conversation on the care center porch, my father died. In my eulogy at his funeral I spoke of him exactly in the way he had spoken of himself that day—as a good and decent man who loved life, loved his family, and who never quit on either. Like the Apostle Paul, he had fought the good fight, had finished the race, and had kept the faith in all he believed in and all that he valued.

While much of what I went on to say is personal and would only be meaningful to his friends and family, I will share my closing words with you because they sum up and will help you to grasp the full importance of having the legacy conversation.

"My question today is not what to do with my grief," I said. "My grief will sort itself out over time. Much like when summer turns to fall, I may not know exactly the time it is fall, but I will know when it is not summer anymore.

"No, my real question today is what to do with my Saturdays. For almost 250 of them, over a five-year span, I ate breakfast with my dad [at his care center], listening to him talk away at first, then watching him gradually fall more and more silent as his memory and the words drifted away. So, I think when this service today is over, and I have rested a bit, I will go back to that place where he spent his final years and find someone just like him, someone whose family doesn't come by as much anymore, whose friends have all forgotten or are dead, yet who has a story to tell if someone will listen.

"I think I will go and listen. I will listen because perhaps when I am old, and the sword I reach for every day is, like me, bent and leaning against a wall, that perhaps the gods who run the universe will look down and say of me too, 'Maybe we should send him someone to bend his ear while they still can. After all, there's nothing like a good story.'"

PART THREE

Implementing
Parent Care Decisions

*Parents are like shuttles on a loom. They join the
threads of the past with threads of the future and leave
their own bright patterns as they go.*
—Fred Rogers, TV's *Mister Rogers*

9

Executing Essential Legal
Documents and Strategies

Decisions and Documents

In the wake of the six conversations you've just had, you and your parents should have made good progress in addressing the eight hundred–pound gorilla in the room that is the parent care issue, and resolving many questions. However, if you still can't get your folks to open up on this issue and provide direction for you, there is not much more you can do except wait for that phone call from the neighbor telling you that your mom has fallen and can't get up or that your dad is walking down the street in his pajamas trying to give away the family dog. At least you now have a heads-up about the psychological, emotional, and financial whirlwind that will follow. Assuming, though, that you have made good progress, you should now be at the point where your parents will need to prepare some legal documents and execute some legal strategies that will enable them to

❖ **Reality Check**

Parental Myth: "My affairs are not complicated; I'll just put down what I want done on a legal pad."

Fact: Parents who believe this are the dream of estate attorneys who specialize in the contesting of wills. One thing that makes America and thirteen other nations (make a game of figuring out which ones) unique on this planet is our sharing of uniform property laws governing who owns and who inherits. In other words, there are guidelines and structures (i.e., documents) for supporting those guidelines, the sole purpose of which is to definitively determine the wishes of the deceased and to carry them out to the letter. Hastily scribbled notes on a legal pad documenting an "uncomplicated" estate plan typically result in vaguely worded wishes and often conflicting promises expressed in semilegible handwriting that lead to lawsuits between surviving family members, the breakup of families, and fat bank accounts for attorneys.

accomplish what they want with a minimum of difficulty and complexity.

As I noted early in the book, the six conversations are the "what" of the parent care solution. These documents and strategies are the "how." Without them, you and your parents will have had some great conversations together but nowhere to go with the decisions that emerged from them. It's like planning the vacation of a lifetime but then not taking it. Let me give you an example.

Brian and Paula Wilson had just retired from their respective careers in dentistry and teaching, and had decided to do some traveling. Brian's dental practice had grown in value substantially over the years. Since his two younger partners had been working under an associate's arrangement wherein Brian owned the practice and they were salaried employees, all three were anxious to replace this arrangement. The Wilsons always visited their attorney to get their affairs in order before they traveled anywhere, so that in the event anything should happen to them, their two daughters and Brian's partners would know what to do.

The attorney drew up the appropriate sales documents, the note securing financing, and the buyout agreement for Brian and his partners to sign, as well as other estate plan documents. The income from the practice note would be a large part of the Wilsons' retirement income, and since Brian owned the building where the dental practice was located, the rental income from the partners would be another source of retirement revenue for him and his wife. In addition, they had money in separate retirement plans as well as a couple of brokerage accounts at a local branch of Bank of America. The intent was for these assets to be overseen by their children, acting together, once they were gone.

After the attorney had drawn up all the documents, the Wilsons decided they would take them home and review them carefully over the weekend before signing them, just to make sure they understood everything. The attorney agreed. These documents, which also included a new will and powers of attorney replacing old ones that had long since been misplaced, were all the Wilsons now had to disburse their assets.

Early Saturday morning, Brian Wilson went for his customary walk. When he returned, he found his wife slumped over the kitchen table, dead from what was later discovered to have

❖ **Reality Check**

Parental Myth: "I can buy some estate planning software and document things myself, less expensively."

Fact: There's a reason that home haircut kits and do-it-your-self brain surgery software have never caught on. Some things are better left to the pros. Estate planning and other legal document software are excellent tools for doing *homework*—for learning what to ask and perhaps even de-ciding what to do about certain issues *before* going to the at-torney, thus saving time and perhaps some money.

been a massive stroke. Overcome with shock and grief, Brian struggled to phone 911, but the stress of the moment caused him to suffer a stroke as well, one that so severely damaged his brain that he expired later that day.

The police notified the Wilsons' children, Grace and Isa-belle, both of whom lived out of town, of their parents' deaths. But due to HIPAA (Health Insurance Portability and Account-ability Act of 1996) regulations, when the women got to the hospital, personnel were prevented from giving them any de-tails about their parents' situation or allowing the bodies to be moved until they could produce sufficient documentation stip-ulating them as next of kin. It took the women almost thirty-six hours to come up with the required proof of who they were. Once they moved their parents' bodies to a local funeral home, they got another shock; they were told that since they were from out of town, the funeral costs (caskets, vaults, gravesites, and preparatory expenses) had to be prepaid to the tune of some $13,000!

Because the Wilsons died intestate (without a will*), their estate ended up being divided equally between their two daughters, but it required nearly a year of bureaucratic red tape and mountains of paperwork to make that happen. Grace and Isabelle inherited their parents' home, personal belongings, and investment accounts, but the latter passed to them minus the tax man's 50 percent bite of the value of the apple due to an unsigned designated beneficiary form.

And then there was the dental practice. Because the note and documents of sale had not been signed, the partners were free to take over the business and pay the daughters a nominal 10 percent of its market value. Furthermore, because the building was in need of some repairs and renovations, the partners were in a good position to bargain over rent; in lieu of turning them out and having to find a new tenant, the daughters were forced to concede them a 50 percent rent reduction to offset the cost of the repairs and improvements they needed to make and to sustain the rent reduction for as long as it took the partners to recoup their expenses.

❖ Reality Check

Parental Myth: "My attorney will make sure all my affairs are in order."

Fact: With or without your help, your parents are responsible for getting their affairs in order, not their attorney. An attorney just drafts the documents, spelling out what your parents want done for them, to sign, and it is that last act of putting their signatures on the dotted line—not the attorney's say-so—that will ensure their affairs are truly in order.

---

*A will had been drawn up but not signed.

Essential Documents and Strategies

Every day in the United States, families, businesses, homes, and fortunes disappear just like that, due to improperly drawn up and/or executed (i.e., signed) legal documents and other papers. It doesn't do any good to go through all the parent care conversations, get into the minutiae of finances and the intimate details of property distribution and legacy goals, only to let the fruit of these discussions—the decisions your parents have made—die on the vine.

The Wilsons had made their care and estate plan decisions; they had gone so far as having the documents drawn up. But then, due to tragic and unforeseen circumstances that left those documents unsigned, many of those decisions could not be executed as they wished, with dire consequences to their children.

The following is a list of the most important care and estate planning documents and related items your parents will need in order to make sure the decisions they've made with your help about their future care and desires will be carried out as they wish. Because all fifty states have different forms, rules, and regulations for these documents, I strongly advise you to consult a legal specialist in your state. While there are various computer programs or do-it-yourself kits that suggest that all you need to do is fill in the blanks, I strongly urge you and your parents to use such programs and kits simply as thinking tools prior to a visit with a legal or tax professional. The areas of law that concern property, care, and possessions overlap and contain potential legal, financial, and tax consequences for the uninformed that may create disastrous results for your family. The local Bar Association or commission may be helpful in directing you to qualified legal, financial, or tax planning preparation in deciding which documents and strategies would serve you best.

Let's take a look at these documents and what they do:

• **Will.** This is really a formal letter from your parents, telling their heirs (such as you) how they want their affairs to be handled after they're gone. A will may be handwritten (often called a holographic will) or more formal (typed by an attorney). It must be witnessed, by as few as two and up to three persons, and sometimes notarized by a notary public as well. Your parents can change their will by creating what's known as a codicil (see Additional Key Documents below) or by writing a new will. A detailed list of their personal property and real estate, specific gifts, or bequests is typically attached to, or included as part of, the will.

• **Declaration of a guardian.** This document allows your parents to select a person (or persons) to look after them and their property or to make important decisions about their personal and business affairs in the event that they become physically or mentally incapacitated and are unable to care for, or make decisions, themselves. If they do not choose a guardian, the courts will appoint one for them should the need arise. If, say, your parents have two children—one of whom is the responsible type (that's you) and the other (your brother) is far too devil-may-care about everything—then choosing wisely themselves is the way to ensure that the courts don't appoint the wrong sibling by default.

• **Powers of attorney.** Powers of attorney allow someone your parents choose to act legally and make decisions on their behalf. These legal and personal powers can be broad and all-encompassing (general power of attorney), narrow and related to one or a few things (limited power of attorney), or reserved for a certain act for a set period of time (special power of attorney). Parents should choose this person carefully and be very sure the person fully understands what he or she is being asked to do. Your parents may set up a power of attorney so they can remove the person (revocable power of attorney) if they feel it necessary or so that the person cannot be removed in the event the parent suffers a serious illness or mental incapacity (irrevocable power of attorney). All powers of attorney cease at issuer's death.

• **Trust.** Think of a trust as sort of a legal lockbox to put assets into. Your parents can create a trust for use while they are alive (living trust) or for after they die (a testamentary trust in their will). A trust can be set up to be undone if or when desired (revocable living trust) or so that it cannot be undone (irrevocable living trust). There are usually three parties involved in the creation of a trust:

1. **Grantor.** The person who puts assets into the trust; i.e., the parents.
2. **Beneficiary.** The person or organization that ultimately gets the assets put into the trust. Beneficiaries may be spouses, children, churches, community organizations, or friends.
3. **Trustee.** The person who watches over the assets in the trust on the grantor's behalf and for the benefit of the beneficiaries. Trustees may be family members, friends, advisors, or institutions such as banks. More than one person may be named as cotrustees.

Different trusts come with a variety of income tax, estate tax, asset protection, privacy, and personal planning advantages that a good trust or estate planning attorney can spell out for you and your parents, to help them design and implement the appropriate trust strategy.

· **Health care power of attorney.** A health care power of attorney gives the person your parent appoints the power to make important decisions concerning their health care and allows that person access to all parties involved with and information related to the parent's medical, hospital, and prescription records and needs. A health care power of attorney is an absolute must in this age of privacy issues and necessary as a practical matter to permit the sharing of a person's medical history and records at critical times under the HIPAA laws. Without having the proper health care powers assigned to them, a person's children, for example, may not be given details about a parent's condition or medical history, particularly if the children are from out of town or trying to obtain that information over the phone, even in an emergency (as was the case with Grace and Isabelle in the tragic story of their folks, the Wilsons). Think of a health care power of attorney as a master key capable of unlocking all the doors to your parents' health care needs. It functions as a sort of

---

❖ Reality Check

Parental Myth: "My old documents are just fine."

Fact: Assuming they really do exist, there is no way those old documents are just fine. In fact, if my twenty-five years of experience as a lawyer serves me at all well here, my guess is that your parents' documents (again, assuming they exist): (1) either don't do what your parents think or want them to do, or (2) were not executed properly to do it. Congress's gyrations over estate tax during the past four years alone are enough to render many estate plan documents drawn up between the Sputnik years and Bosnia either outdated or extinct.

universal permission slip giving the person possessing it the ability to talk to anyone, consult with anyone, or collaborate with anyone to ensure that their loved one's health care requirements and wishes are met.

Additional Key Documents

The following is a list of other documents parents may want to discuss with their attorney in arranging their legal affairs. A board-certified estate planning attorney or other professional specializing in Medicare, Medicaid, or elder care planning (such as an elder care attorney) will help determine which, if any, of these additional documents may be needed.

• **Affidavit of domicile.** This is a signed statement affirming the individual is a resident of the state, jurisdiction, city, or county that he or she claims to be. It is used as proof of residence in many legal situations as well as when applying for a driver's license, veteran's benefits, or in processing a Medicaid claim.

• **Change of beneficiary letter.** This notifies the individual's life insurance company of his or her intent to change beneficiaries on the policy. The legal impact is that the change becomes irrevocable. Therefore, make sure from the attorney creating this letter that changing the beneficiary (or beneficiaries) will not have dire tax consequences. Making the estate (rather than one's spouse, for example) the new beneficiary will result in all that insurance money being taxable upon the individual's death.

• **Codicil to the will.** This is a change to an existing will, which functions as an additional instruction to the executor. A codicil can be used to alter all or part of a will. If improperly drafted, it can have the effect of disavowing the previous will entirely, whether desired or not. Typically, one adds a codicil as the result of an afterthought or a desire to insert some minor change—for example, including someone not previously named in the will for a small amount or excluding someone else. It is usually wise to have an attorney draw up a codicil or draft a completely new will if the changes are extensive.

• **DNR (do not resuscitate).** This form is placed in the medical file of a terminally ill individual at the request of that individual, instructing medical personnel to take no measures to restore the person's breathing once it has stopped.

• **Employee death benefits letter.** A lawyer or executor of an estate sends this to an employer as notification of the employee's death, and requesting a payout of all benefits entitled to the deceased or to his or her beneficiaries. The benefits payable in response to this type of document would include the proceeds from an individual or group life insurance policy, a burial benefit, the balance of any disability benefits, or residual payments from a pension or profit sharing plan. Any accrued but unused paid vacation as well as any deferred bonus or compensation may be made payable as an employee benefit, as well.

• **Health care power of attorney revocation.** This document takes away the authority given the holder to act on the grantor's behalf regarding health care matters.

• **Letter to successor trustee.** A grantor creates a trust and appoints a trustee to watch over its content. According to the terms of the trust agreement, however, the trustee may be terminated or choose to resign and a successor trustee appointed. If that occurs, this letter announces the appointment of the successor trustee and grants him or her the full powers of the original trustee.

- **Letter to the executor.** This is prepared as part of an estate plan and is usually filed or kept with other documents such as the will, power of attorney, health care directives, and so on. It serves to amplify, reaffirm, or create anew certain instructions the executor is being asked to perform on behalf of the deceased.

- **Living will.** Many times referred to as the "respirator will," this is a directive by a severely ill person requesting that no extraordinary means be taken to sustain his or her life at the expense of the quality of that life should the illness take a dramatic turn for the worse.

- **Medical claims form.** This is filed either by an individual, or on behalf of that individual if he or she is deceased, for reimbursement of any out-of-pocket medical expenses. It is usually filed with the person's employer, or in the case of self-employed individuals, with the insurer providing the coverage.

- **Medical records transfer form.** Very often life insurance companies will require a complete file on an individual's medical history before issuing a life insurance or disability insurance policy or claim. A primary physician or health care provider usually provides these forms. They are necessary when requesting that medical records or medical information on an individual be transferred to another provider or given to someone (son or daughter, for example) requesting that certain medical benefits be paid or that certain medical procedures be performed.

- **Memorial plan.** This is a letter describing how the individual wants his or her services to be conducted when the time comes. It covers choice of music and location, number of participants and eulogies, and so on. It can be a single sheet of paper with as much or as little detail as desired. For lifelong control freaks, it is a way to script and direct the final scene in the third act of their life's drama.

- **Notice of death to insurance company.** The executor uses this document to inform the life insurance company of the policyholder's death so that benefits will be released to the beneficiary. A life insurance company will usually require a certified copy of the death certificate and sometimes even a photocopy of the deceased's driver's license or birth certificate, to substantiate the executor's authorization and request. Typically, it is filed within a few weeks after the policyholder's death.

- **Notice to terminate joint account.** A request to a financial institution such as a bank, brokerage firm, or insurance company to transfer the account or financial instrument in question either into another joint tenant, tenant in common, tenant by the entirety, or individual account. The purpose is stop one or both of the holders from keeping withdrawal and other privileges on contents of the account.

- **Request for life insurance claim form.** A written notice to the insurance company asking that all documentation relevant to the deceased's life insurance contract is forwarded to the executor, beneficiary, or legal representative so that a proceeds letter may follow.

- **Request for life insurance proceeds letter.** The executor of the estate, the deceased's beneficiary, or a legal representative files this with the insurance company to claim the proceeds from a policy taken out on the deceased's life. In most cases, a certified copy of the death certificate must accompany it.

- **Request for death certificate.** Though some jurisdictions will allow a notarized written request, typically a request for a death certificate must be made in person at the courthouse where the deceased's public records are kept. A request for a death certificate is usually made when proof is required, in processing insurance and hospital reimbursement claims and the like, that the deceased is, in fact, deceased.

• **Revocation of power of attorney.** This document rescinds a grantor's permission to act on his or her behalf, often due to a disagreement over the way the grantor's affairs are being handled. It can also be used by the holder to give up the power of attorney to someone else if he or she is no longer up to performing, or no longer wants to perform, the duties required.

• **Self-proving affidavit.** As the word *affidavit* means "to affirm" or to acknowledge as true, this document attests to the accuracy of all information stated within by the individual about him or herself and his or her situation.

• **Social Security application form.** This is filed with the Social Security Administration six months in advance of the individual's start date in order to begin receiving benefits.

• **Social Security change form.** This is used either to request a change in the date benefits start, to stop benefits, or to change the name of the individual to whom the benefits are made payable. Such a change may be needed in the event the person becomes ill, can no longer handle his or her affairs, or is declared legally incompetent.

• **Stock power.** This gives the executor of the estate (or whomever is named to act on the deceased's behalf) the authority to buy or sell stocks owned by a decedent. The document instructs the brokerage firm or agency holding the stock certificates that the deceased owner has transferred his or her power to trade the stock to someone else. It must be notarized, and post-9/11 requires authentication of the identity of the individual, executor, estate, or personal representative given this power.

• **Veteran's request for information.** Sent to the Veteran's Administration in Washington, DC, by or on behalf of a qualifying individual to claim his or her veteran's benefits.

Choosing Advisors—the Critical Questions to Ask

The health care system in the United States is an amalgam of often-contradictory advice and crossed paths. Forget about the vagaries of Medicare and Medicaid, just sorting through the care facility options almost requires a degree in social work or geriatric case management. When you have to consider the options of at-home medical care versus at-home nonmedical care with filtering your care facility questions (see chapter 7, "The Professional Care Conversation") through the different privacy acts and the HIPAA regulations governing access to your parents' personal records, the average human being is tempted to drop his or her parents off at the emergency room in the middle of the night and just drive away. In fact, I suspect that as our population ages, we will see more and more grown children resorting to extreme options to facilitate their aging parents' care.

The yellow pages of the phone book will list all the legal, financial, and health care professionals in your area who are ready and willing to help you and your parents to sort through the paperwork and other complexities of their future care and estate planning situation. But are these professionals able, as well? You won't find the answer to that in the yellow pages. You will have to do some questioning yourself.

Here are the *essential questions* to ask any potential legal, financial, or health care advisor you may be considering to help with strategizing and executing your parents' wishes. Following each question, rate your degree of satisfaction with the advisor's response by circling one of the following numbers: 5 for "extremely satisfied," 4 for "very satisfied," 3 for "somewhat satisfied," 2 for "somewhat dissatisfied," and 1 for "keep looking!"

Then check the score at the end to determine the advisor's overall pass/fail grade.

The Parent Care Conversation Essential Advisor Questions

1. **What is the advisor's *primary* business?** The answer to this will tell you exactly what expertise the advisor brings to the table so that you will be able to determine what additional expertise and support you may need—and whether the advisor has access to that expertise and support. Let's face it, in this complex world nobody has *all* the answers. If the advisor is *primarily* a geriatric caseworker or an elder care attorney, you will still need the assistance of other professionals to design and execute your care plan. 5   4   3   2   1

2. **How long has the advisor been in business?** Every professional advisor merits at least a try-out client, but you don't want to be the one. It is possible for a law student to make it all way through law school without ever having to take a course in wills or trusts or income taxes. Just because the advisor has a credential doesn't mean he or she has the experience and competence to go with it. 5   4   3   2   1

3. **What was the last seminar the advisor attended in his or her field?** What you are looking for here is a commitment to learning, growth, and progress in the subject the advisor professes to be his or her life's work. Every occupation offers conferences, continuing education, and opportunities for professional advancement. If the advisor is an estate planning attorney but the only seminars he or she attends are on flower arranging, and he or she can't come up with another book read since *Danny and the Steam Shovel*, be cautious! 5   4   3   2   1

4. **Is the advisor willing to offer references?** What you're looking for here is feedback about the advisor from some of his or her clients just like you that will fall along the continuum of:

❖ TIP! A Bias for Action

Remember the story of the Wilsons at the beginning of this chapter? Perhaps at least some of the catastrophes that befell their children might have been prevented if the Wilsons' attorney had insisted they sign the documents he'd drawn up before leaving his office rather than taking them with them—especially given their pending travel plans. Nothing happens until someone makes it happen. Choose an advisor with a bias for action, not one who just goes along or who is afraid to ruffle the client's feathers when things aren't getting done fast enough.

"He (or she) is the most incredible, empathetic, intelligent, up-to-the-minute, aware, connected, totally interfaced advisor on the planet" to "Yes, I would buy a used car from this person." Beware the advisor who hems and haws over this question or absolutely refuses your request. When prospective clients ask me if they can talk to some of my current clients about me, my response is always that I will be happy to open that door when I am on their short list and not just someone they are "considering." I've found that my clients are more than willing to help me acquire others just like them by offering such feedback; I just don't want them bugged by people who are not serious. Here's a helpful hint: don't ask to invade the privacy of the advisor's client list unless you are very serious about hiring the person. If you do become a client, there may be a day when someone solicits you for feedback, and the last thing you will want is that someone calling you on a Sunday afternoon just to do some tire-kicking and price-shopping. 5 4 3 2 1

5. What is the worst thing a client has ever said about the advisor? The advisor's response to this question will tell you how much of a straight shooter he or she is—because if the answer is "nothing," this indicates perfection, which doesn't exist. Some of my clients have said that I am "impatient," that I "talk too fast," and that I sometimes "don't pay enough attention to them." This is all very true of me, though I would add that it is true of me only with clients who stay too long, never listen, and whine constantly. But I'm willing to say it. 5 4 3 2 1

6. How does the advisor see the two of you working together? This is a great question because it lets you know how the advisor approaches setting goals and achieving objectives on your behalf. Look for the response to reveal both an interest in and an understanding of your situation as well as the role the advisor can play in responding to it. If, for example, the advisor mentions your situation and the newest model Porsche in the same sentence, use caution and proceed slowly. 5 4 3 2 1

7. How would working with you improve the advisor professionally? You should be able to detect from the advisor's response to this whether there is something of real interest to him or her, something stimulating about your situation that gets the advisor's professional juices flowing. And I don't mean the prospect

---

❖ TIP! Beware Charisma

Don't handicap the compensation area just because you're swayed by charisma. I am suspect of charisma when interviewing any professional advisor, but especially in situations where there are mutual funds involved or new-business development officers are present at the meeting.

of a fatter bank account. It might be that the advisor values the relationship and the ability to help and solve problems, or that certain technical complications must be mastered to move forward in solving your particular problem, and the advisor likes the excitement of the challenge this presents. You will know if it's just a big check the advisor is looking for if he or she goes quickly to the discount conversation. You want an interested and enthused advisor, not one that just answers roll call. 5   4   3   2   1

8. **Will you be working with the advisor, an associate, or a team?** The answer to this question will establish the expectations you have now and in the future. Many professionals, in all fields, are good at initial meetings but terrible on follow-through without associates or a team to back them up and delegate the details to. If they have no such backup, you may be doomed. On the other hand, having backup should not excuse them from being available when necessary. Helpful hint: if the person you are talking to in the initial meeting is just the new-business development manager, ask to see an organizational chart and to talk to the people on the team who will be directly handling your case. 5   4   3   2   1

9. **What does the advisor charge, and how?** Get it right out on the table, what you will be charged and how the advisor is to be compensated. Will charges be on an hourly basis? If so, what is the rate per hour and how many hours does the advisor estimate his or her involvement will take? Does the advisor charge a flat fee? If so, what does the fee arrangement cover? If the person is a financial advisor, is he or she being compensated on assets under management? If so, what is the percentage you will be charged? If compensation is for the sale of commissionable products such as life insurance, health insurance, long-term care insurance, or annuities, what is the commission paid, and what are similar products paying? Right now, the only people

that are faced with more disclosure rules than the financial services industry are those going through intake at the county
lockup—and for similar reasons. Today, lack of transparency
and full disclosure by anyone in the financial services will result
in a felony count. 5 4 3 2 1

❖ TIP! You Get What You Pay For

Beware the low-cost provider. Rule of thumb: estate law
and anesthesiology are two fields where you definitely don't
want the discounter.

---

10. **How accessible and available will the advisor be?** I always tell my clients that while I may not always be available, I am
accessible. That may not be enough for some clients, who expect
the advisor to always be at their beck and call. I, for one, am not
willing to interrupt or miss meetings with other clients, or to be
unable to spend time with my family or engage in other important activities in order to do that. However, I am always willing to
be accessible to my clients—and immediately available *under certain conditions and circumstances,* such as an IRS agent at the
client's doorstep with a subpoena or an invitation to meet with a
grand jury. When advisors tell you they personally are available
24/7/365, you can bet they don't have enough resources, opportunities, or experience not to be. 5 4 3 2 1

11. **Is there anything the advisor would like to ask *you*?**
Good advisors should have a similar list of questions they will
want to cover with you. In fact, if they're really good, they'll
have their own version of the CARE system to help them query
you about the challenges you are facing that brought you to

them; the alternatives you are considering; the resources you have to pay them and to implement their advice; and, finally, the experience you would like to have as the result of hiring them if everything works out right. 5   4   3   2   1

❖ Rate the Advisor

Add up the grades you gave the advisor in response to the questions; then divide the total by the number of questions on the list (eleven). The average you get will fall somewhere between one and five. Apply the same "extremely satisfied" to "keep looking!" rating definitions used in the questionnaire to determine the advisor's overall grade. For example, let's say the total score you gave the advisor is thirty-five. Divide that by the number of questions asked (thirty-five divided by eleven) and you come up with an overall grade for the potential advisor of 3.2, or "somewhat satisfied" bordering on "very satisfied," which makes that advisor a better-than-average potential candidate.

How Long Will It Take?

You and your parents have gone through all six conversations and come up with all the information and decisions necessary to satisfy the three of you. You know what your parents' view of the future is, you know where all their assets are located, they've decided on the family home versus Merry Acres, everybody's content with where and/or to whom all the surplus socks and underwear go, and you know how your parents want to be remembered. How long, then, should it take to prepare, sign, and have the documents in place and ready to be executed when the time comes to ensure your parents' wishes are carried out?

Excluding the time it may take to find a legal and/or financial advisor to help and assuming you and your parents have the advisor in place, in a nonemergency situation, thirty to ninety days is a realistic time frame to complete all the important care and estate plan documents described in this chapter. The actual consolidation and transfer of financial information on some type of aggregate platform should not take longer than the same thirty to ninety days. Conceivably, everything can be in place within three months of having the parent care conversations and making all or most of your parents' future care and estate plan decisions.

As with almost everything else in life, organization is the key to implementation. Based on the care decisions your parents have made, help them to create a checklist (see the Document Directory Checklist Tool below) of each care and estate plan document that needs to be drawn up, when the document is completed, and when it has been signed, so that nothing will fall through the cracks.

The Parent Care Solution Document Directory Checklist Tool

The following information should be easily located and accessible to the holder of your power of attorney. Complete account numbers, phone numbers, and addresses should be noted whenever possible.

Document	Done	Date	Location
CPA			
Lawyer			
Auto title			
Home title			

Document	Done	Date	Location
Deeds			
Bank account			
Brokerage accounts			
Credit card accounts			
Employer information			
Insurance agent			
Insurance policies			
Medicare, Medicaid, health insurance cards			
Pastor, minister, priest, rabbi			
Mortgage papers			
Passport			
Physicians			
Dentists			
Ophthalmologist			
Social Security			
Investment advisor			
Financial planner			
Banker			
General power of attorney			
Health care power of attorney			

Record Keeping

There's an old story about the governmental agency that, when faced with a lack of any more storage room for keeping records, made the decision to destroy every file older than five years to free up more space and to make copies of them! Record keeping at home follows a similar pattern. We become pack rats. How do we know what to keep and what to shred? The following Important Documents Timeline Tool lists the key records and the time frames for holding on to them.

Two biggies are bank records and tax returns. One is usually needed to resolve a dispute with the other. The short lesson here: if you think you may need it, you probably will. Tax returns—yes. Twenty years of Utah Power and Light bills—no. Note: this tool applies to paper documents only. In the digital age, virtually everything is retrievable at almost any time.

The Parent Care Solution Important Documents Timeline Tool

Document	How Long?	Why?
Tax return	six years	IRS can audit within three years if it suspects a filing error. Same applies if you file an amended return. IRS has six years for 25 percent understatement of income.
Canceled checks	six years	Just because
Brokerage statements	six years	Same as IRS; for IRS backup
Mutual funds statements		
Bank statements		

Document	How Long?	Why?
Real estate	six years	IRS backup
Paycheck stubs	six years	IRS backup Also save final pay stub of year for cumulative withholding information.
Credit cards	six years	IRS backup, especially if business purchases have been made.
Retirement plan data	six years	Quarterly statements until end of year. The annual statement.

Meet the Jamisons

OK, so what might a future care and estate plan look like if, unlike the Wilsons, your parents had actually followed through on their decisions with signed, sealed, and ready-to-execute documents and strategies? To find out, let's meet the Jamisons.

Bill and Susan Jamison are in their seventies and have just completed the parent care conversations. During these conversations, they discovered a great deal about themselves and their relationship with their four children. For example, they were delighted to discover that contrary to their belief that they were just a burden to the children, their kids actually welcomed the opportunity to help them. And the children discovered that the same fiscal prudence that had enabled their parents to provide all four of them with a college education had also enabled their parents to put more than enough away in investments and real estate to ensure their income would continue for the rest of their lives. Life insurance made sure that if either one of them died prematurely there would be enough money for the surviving spouse, and the life insurance would shift the cost of care during the most expensive years onto the insurance company. Although this long-term care policy had seemed expensive when the Jamisons purchased it, the premiums were a fraction of what the policy would pay for care if the need arose.

With their house paid for as well as their automobiles, the Jamisons were ready to implement some of the decisions they had made.

The first thing they did was sign the wills their attorney had prepared. Because the size of their estate was not huge, these were not complicated documents. They executed what are called "I love you" wills leaving everything to the surviving spouse. At the time of the second spouse's death (or in the event of simultaneous deaths), the remaining assets were to be divided equally among the four children. If there were a disagreement among the children, the Jamisons' attorney would be the final arbiter whose power was absolute.

The Jamisons transferred the title to their home to a trust they created for the children, reserving a "life estate" in their home, which gave them the right to live there as long as they wanted and were able. Under the terms of the trust agreement, the children were free to tap into the home's equity if necessary for their parents' care. The children decided to use a portion of the equity to purchase additional life insurance on their parents and, at the same time, purchased credit insurance on the mortgage. This way, when their parents died, any equity line balance would be paid in full and the children would inherit the house free and clear. The Jamisons had also taken full advantage of the Parent Care Cost-Recovery System (see chapter 4, "The Money

Conversation," for full details) to help the children recover any out-of-pocket money for their parents' care, as well.

After each other, the Jamisons nominated the two oldest children to be holders of their general powers of attorney, followed by the younger siblings as necessary. If no children were available, the local bank was to be the trustee for the Jamisons' affairs. They followed the same strategy for their health care powers of attorney. But here, if the children were unavailable to make the decisions, a three-party committee of the Jamisons' lawyer, accountant, and family physician were to make these decisions. The Jamisons also executed living wills in conjunction with the health care power of attorney, giving these individuals the right to decline or cease the use of life-support services or extraordinary medical care to prolong the Jamisons' lives in the event of a terminal illness.

Their accountant suggested a family investment company for the Jamisons' liquid assets. Under this arrangement, their investment holdings were transferred to a limited liability company (LLC) where Bill and Susan were members, but their children were the *managing* members having all rights of distribution. This strategy—which they initiated for legitimate personal and business reasons and not to defraud the Medicaid system—protected the Jamisons' current assets and the inheritance for the children from the Medicaid rules allowing the system to look back for a period of ten years to offset monies expended for the recipient's care by the state's Medicaid program.

The additional life insurance policies were transferred to the Jamisons' irrevocable life insurance trust with the children as beneficiaries. The children were empowered to make the premium payments using either income from the family investment company assets or the equity line on the house. At the parents' deaths, the insurance proceeds from the policy would go into the trust and then could be distributed to the surviving children or grandchildren.

The Jamisons' automobiles were also placed in the LLC, an action that enabled the children to buy, sell, or otherwise dispose of the vehicles as needs arose. Policy limits on both automobiles were increased to the maximum liability levels. The LLC also purchased an umbrella liability policy to protect assets in the event the Jamisons suffered a traffic accident and the judgment exceeded the amounts covered by their auto policies.

There were some personal items Bill and Susan Jamison wanted the children to have: Bill's pocket watch, his Scout knife, Susan's wedding rings, and her fiftieth wedding anniversary diamond necklace, which were all bequeathed in a separate document attached to the will.

Finally, Bill, Susan, and the children together decided to create a family crypt at a local mausoleum and to prepay for services. They also created a family legacy video to be passed on, consisting of snapshots of Bill, Susan, and the children as the family grew over the years. Also, the in-depth talks about their lives the Jamisons had with their children during the legacy conversation were recorded for posterity. Each child would receive a copy of the video at the death of the parents, in order to preserve their memory.

The Jamisons' story is a far cry from that of the Wilsons, which began this chapter, isn't it? If the Wilsons had carried out even a percentage of the strategies the Jamisons did with regard to their future care and estate plans, many of the dire events that befell the Wilsons' children upon the premature and tragic deaths of their parents could have been positively turned around.

Is it necessary for every family to do everything the Jamisons did? Probably not. But everything the Jamisons did is available to every family, and, therefore, should be considered as part of any parent care and estate plan solution.

As the baby boomers age and continue to reinvent the whole notion of retirement and aging, there will likely be even more innovations like those the Jamisons used and even greater capabilities for carrying out the wishes of our aging parents and preserving family relationships and finances. Stay tuned to the parent care conversation Web site (www.parentcaresolution.com) for updates and news you can use on this key issue.

❖ DOs and DON'Ts

DO make sure that everyone who should be involved in the documenting phase *is* involved.

DO plan enough ahead to allow for making any changes and corrections before you actually need the document.

DO store important documents where key people can easily find them.

DO tell those key people where the important documents are.

DO create a checklist of all documents signed and the dates.

DON'T put this off.

DON'T rest until every document is signed and ready to be executed.

DON'T make any changes to your documents without telling your attorney.

10

Staying On Top of Things

A Work in Progress

Any future care plan, no matter how well thought out and designed, is inevitably a work in progress due to the unpredictability of life. We never know what punches life will throw at us, which makes it all the more important that we anticipate those punches as much as possible and are able to roll with them. Otherwise, what happened to the Stedman family could happen to yours.

Walter Stedman was a self-made man living in Rosemont, a suburb of Chicago. His wife, Eleanor, died four years ago from lung cancer. Walter had been managing for himself since, in the home he and his late wife had occupied throughout their almost fifty years of marriage. During Eleanor's illness it became apparent to both of them that they should discuss their future plans with their children, who lived in Indianapolis, Indiana, about a four-hour drive away. Walter and Eleanor had designed a parent care strategy. With the help of their advisors, their financial affairs were in order, their estate plan was organized, their family home was protected, and their health care directives were all signed and executed. Thus, while Eleanor's death came as no less of a shock to the family, it was made less chaotic by the plans the Stedmans had put in place. For example, they had planned for Walter to be able to stay in his home for as long as he chose and then to move to a nearby retirement village.

❖ Reality Check

Parental Myth: "My body needs a checkup now and then, but my care plan doesn't. It's all set."

Fact: A lot can happen between the time your parents make decisions about their future and the time that future arrives and those decisions kick in. Any parent care solution worth its salt is a living structure; it must be flexible enough to accommodate whatever changes will arise in your parents' needs and wishes as time goes by and their situation evolves.

After his wife's death, Walter began seeing Elizabeth, a widow, whom he met at a seniors' social. He eventually asked her to move in with him, and she did. During the years they had together, before Walter's own health began to deteriorate, Elizabeth assumed more and more of the day-to-day housekeeping responsibilities, functioning more like a wife than just a companion. Walter authorized her signature on his personal checking, savings, and investment accounts. While this did not legally name her as holder of those accounts, her signature authority effectively created the same situation. As the relationship developed between them, they began to commingle their monies on a more frequent basis. He would put money into her checking account, she would write checks on his for joint items, and they would jointly share the cost of things such as vacations and gifts or going out with friends. He even gave her a Rolex watch to wear that had belonged to his late wife.

A year before Walter Stedman died, he went to an attorney (not the same one he and his late wife had used) to re-form the deed and title to the house to make Elizabeth co-owner with him. He was worried that if he died or became ill and had to move to a professional care facility, she would have nowhere to live. Six months later, he sat down one evening with Elizabeth and wrote out a new will by hand, revoking an earlier will drawn up by his original attorney. This time, he left everything to Elizabeth except for a few items earmarked for his children. He spelled out everything so there would be no confusion as to who got what.

Only after his death did his children discover his actions and come to realize the depth of feeling their father had for Elizabeth. They immediately challenged the legitimacy of the handwritten will as well as Elizabeth's entitlements to their father's retirement, checking, and brokerage accounts, demanding that all monies she had taken be returned in whole to those accounts. Elizabeth refused to do this, or to leave the house, so the children filed suit against her, asking that the title to the house and everything else be restored to them as their father's rightful heirs, including their mother's Rolex watch and other jewelry.

A trial was held and the judge upheld the transfer of title to the family home to Elizabeth, stating there was no evidence that Walter had made the transfer under duress or undue influence, a fact that was confirmed by the new attorney Walter had used. In the matter of the Rolex (and other jewelry of his late wife's that Walter had given to Elizabeth), the judge ruled that she could keep what Walter had given her but was not permitted to receive any other jewelry left in the estate that had belonged to the late Eleanor Stedman. Finally, the judge ruled that while the addition of Elizabeth's signature authority on Walter's various accounts did not constitute "absolute title," the fact that she had the authority to write checks on those accounts did give her "constructive title," and he thus awarded all liquid assets and investment assets in the accounts to her. As a result, the two Stedman children were left with very little of their parents' estate. This was certainly not what their mother had wanted; in fact, it was what the original documents drawn up by their parents had sought to avoid.

It is likely that this turn of events is not what their father had wanted to happen either, but he had virtually ensured it would happen nonetheless by keeping the true nature of his relationship with Elizabeth a virtual secret from his children and not revising and updating his estate documents in line with the original strategy he and his late wife had designed. In fact, he didn't even tell his new attorney there was such as plan! He went boldly, and foolishly, off on his own without considering the fact that Elizabeth had children of her own. By making her heir, he had inadvertently shut out his own kids.

Staying On Track

The moral of the Stedman story is that once a care plan has been successfully designed and the relevant documents drawn up, it is only the beginning. It is still necessary to review and update strategies and documents as needed to accommodate changes that have occurred since the original care plan was designed and to anticipate any changes that may occur in the future. Furthermore, all interested parties (spouses, children, advisors) should be kept fully in the loop!

Here's how to keep what happened to the Stedman family from happening to yours.

Review Decisions Periodically

You will recall from earlier chapters my emphasis on the importance of confidence in transforming fear into focused thinking, communication, and action. That's what the parent care conversations do—they help your parents develop the confidence to make decisions and move forward. Holding onto that confidence is just as important because change, no matter how slight—but especially sudden or unanticipated change—can totally destroy your parents' confidence about the direction they are heading, unless they have an appropriate way of dealing with potential change.

At least once a year, your parents should review (with your help and/or that of the conversation facilitator) any material changes that have occurred in their lives during that time that might cause them to rethink any plans or decisions they have made regarding their future care. For example, as a result of the house conversation, your parents may have decided they intend to stay in their home as long as possible, but suddenly your dad's ability to move about the house has been significantly affected due to a stroke or the onset of a chronic illness. In light of this dramatic change, it may be time to revisit the house conversation and come up with a plan B.

Typically, over the course of a year the most fluctuating changes in a person's circumstances or situation, including the elderly, occur in the financial realm. Because the money conversation is the most involved of the six parent care conversations, I have created a separate review structure for parents to use in addressing any changes that have occurred in their financial situation and to rethink decisions they've made in that area so they can react quickly and effectively to them. A more general structure follows for use as a template in reviewing the five other areas of the parent care conversations, from housing and professional care decisions to property issues. Both review structures follow a similar, easy-to-use Q&A format.

The goal of an annual parent care conversation review is to get parents to:

- Examine their original thinking on the major strategic areas they need to focus on
- Reflect on changes that have occurred (or may occur) within those strategic areas
- Incorporate any changes in their own thinking or situation that have made, or would make, them reconsider aspects of their original plan

My Future Care Decisions— Money Conversation Review

Your parents should respond precisely to each question within each category and take action with their advisor in updating plan documents and details accordingly.

1. **Cash Flow Planning**
   a. What amount of cash is in reserve and readily accessible for income or emergency needs?

b. Has there been an increase in cash flow needs over the past year? How much and under what circumstances?

c. What are major outlays that may occur in the next twelve months that weren't part of my original plan?

d. What am I earning on my cash reserves? Are there other places to invest?

2. **Income Tax Planning**

a. Are my estimated taxes current with last year's?

b. Should I increase or decrease my estimated tax payments or withholdings?

c. Can any taxable distributions be offset with care expenses?

d. Are there any possible medical equipment deductions that can be taken?

3. **Insurance Planning**

a. Is all my life, health, disability, major medical, and long-term care coverage up-to-date, at maximum affordable levels, and competitively priced?

b. Is there coverage I should increase, decrease, or let lapse?

c. Have all my deductibles been met for the year?

4. **Investment Planning**

a. If now taking distributions, what is the ratio of my withdrawals to earnings, and am I starting to draw down on principal?

b. Am I balancing my taxable versus nontaxable investments?

c. What is my return relative to my goals and objectives?

d. Is my portfolio balanced and operating efficiently for my goals and objectives?

5. **Retirement Planning**

a. If retired, how do my income and expenses relate to each other?

b. If considering retirement, how will my portfolio make or prohibit that opportunity?

c. Am I doing more of the things in retirement that I want to and less of what I don't want to?

6. **Estate Planning**

a. Are all my documents signed and capable of doing what I want them to?

b. What changes do I need to make because of new laws?

c. What changes do I want to make regardless of the laws?

My Future Care Decisions—General Review

Parents should use this template for reviewing each of the other five areas of the parent care conversations (big picture, property, house, professional care, and legacy) annually in light of any changes that may have occurred in those areas during the course of a year:

1. What are the changes that have occurred in this area since we did our original thinking and planning?

2. What changes do we want to make regardless of any changes that may or may not have occurred?

3. What new challenges have arisen in this particular area that we must now face? What challenges do we no longer have to face?

4. What new alternatives or options have presented themselves in dealing with these challenges? What alternatives or options previously available to us no longer are?

5. What new resources are available to us for maximizing our options in this area? What resources are no longer available to us in our current situation?

6. What about the experience we would like to have in this area would we now prefer to be different? What about the experience we would like to have in this area might now have to change?

Rebound Quickly, Strategically, and with Focus

In some of its components, a parent care plan is a lot like an emergency kit. You buy it hoping that when the time comes to use it, it will be for a cut or a scrape and not major surgery. Mostly, though, there will not be much to do except implement the decisions called for by the plan when the moment comes. As with a good emergency kit, the fundamentals are all there. This will make it easier to rebound in those situations where, for example, a sudden change in your parents' health dictates a fast response.

Once your parents move from their home to a professional care facility, such as a retirement community or assisted-living complex, the reality is that their health is what motivated the move, so additional changes in their health will become, more and more, a situation that you will have to react to quickly. With certain diseases of the elderly, such as Parkinson's or Alzheimer's, there are peaks and valleys and plateaus as the diseases run their course. There will be periods of time when it seems that you are responding to changes on almost a weekly, even a daily, basis, and other periods when it seems like nothing noticeable changes at all.

More often than not, the changes that occur will require consultation with health care professionals attending to your parents' care. During my father's time in assisted living, for example, it seemed to me that I was constantly dealing with decisions about medicine changes, doctor visits, treatment regimens, or physical therapy and exercise. Each decision required a new level of attention and focus. The documents you and your parents will have put in place, such the general and health care powers of attorney, will make it far less difficult for you to acquire the information you need to reach that new level of attention and focus, so you can respond knowledgably, strategically, and swiftly.

Anticipate and Adapt

There is an axiom of war that all battle plans change once the first shot is fired. While a parent care plan is light years beyond the alternative of digging one's head in the sand and just reacting to events as they occur, even the most carefully designed parent care plan cannot address *everything* that is likely to happen as your parents enter the twilight period of their lives. There will be times when the impact of external forces will make you feel as though you are winging it. Adaptability is key here. These are some of the external forces you can safely assume will throw a monkey wrench into any well-designed plan, so that you can anticipate and adapt quickly to them:

• **Governmental regulations.** Unless you've just arrived on the planet, you have to be aware of the massive tremors that are starting to shake the structures of Medicare and Medicaid, not to mention Social Security. The truth about these programs is that while they are well-intentioned, with a noble purpose, they have grown into huge entitlement programs that consume increasingly larger and larger portions of the federal budget. Even if certain pressures on those programs were not there, what you have is a sort of national health insurance program that has been funded by the contributions of those still working. The problem as our population ages is that we will have more people demanding services from those programs than we have people working to fund them. This won't happen all at once, but over the next twenty years look for some major changes in the way money and care will be meted out by these two systems. This goes for Social Security as well. Social Security began as a safety net program designed to keep our citizens from falling into abject poverty as they got older by giving them a minimal level of subsistence to live on in their retirement years. But it has now become a default retirement plan for millions of Americans. While it is unlikely that Social Security will ever be dissolved completely, it is very likely that the current structure of the program will not be the same for you (depending upon your age) and definitely not for your children as it was for the World War II generation. Whether by indexing, or age-based selection, Social Security as we know it will not sustain future generations nor will the belief that it can fiscally survive, certainly in its present form, much beyond the last wave of retiring baby boomers. I tell my parent care clients this: the government is getting out of the retirement business, and that means you should be getting into it by taking responsibility right now, wherever you are, whatever your age and state of health, for the sound fiscal prognosis of your future care and well-being.

• **Rising health care costs.** The American Medical Association and the National Trial Lawyers Association each blames the other for rising health care costs. Doctors blame trial lawyers for multimillion-dollar medical negligence verdicts. Trial lawyers blame doctors for sloppy medical practices that allegedly injure, kill, and mutilate thousands of people annually. And all the while, hospitals blame both sides, and the drug companies, for increased operating costs. Well, guess what? They're all correct, at least partially. To some degree they are all responsible for rising costs. Health care *is* expensive to administer and deliver in our society, with or without negligence and lawsuits. It's expensive because we have come to expect, almost as our right, access to the highest quality medical care, delivered to us on a just-in-time basis by the most highly skilled practioners available in state-of-the-art medical care facilities. What about that suggests even the prospect of a discount or decrease in health care costs coming soon? Rising health care costs are one of the most predictable of all changes that will impact any parent care plan. It is estimated that roughly 20 percent of the health care costs in a person's life are incurred in the last three months of life. The average annual cost of a nursing home stay is in excess of $73,000 per year and rising at the rate of 8–12 percent per annum. To stay on top of this aspect of the care plan you and your parents have designed, increased health care costs as your parents age must be expected and planned for *now,* with the assets and resources you have available *now.* This is why the money conversation (see chapter 4) is so important and why an annual review of the financial decisions that come out of that conversation is so critical.

· **Low or unpredictable portfolio returns.** What the 1990s gave to us in superior investment performance, the first years of the twenty-first century have all but taken away. A dollar in the equity markets is worth three cents *less* as I write this in September 2005 than it was worth in September 2000. That is, of course, if none of that dollar had to be withdrawn to live on during that same period, in which case it is worth even less today. For most of our parents' working lives, and our own, investors have been projecting the average growth rate in equities as between 6 percent and 8 percent on the conservative side, 8–12 percent on the moderately conservative side, and 12–15 percent on the aggressive side. Based on these assumptions, the thinking has been that we could safely withdraw 5 percent from the value of our portfolios to live on if the principal at least remained stable (it surely wouldn't drop.) Not true. In fact, one of the changes you will have to anticipate in today's market environment is an average 3–5 percent growth rate, conservatively speaking, with a 2–3 percent withdrawal rate. Those percentages are a far cry from the projections most financial advisors in the early to late 1990s said were possible. My advice to today's children of aging parents: do not assume an overly aggressive rate of return from your parents' portfolios to make up for rising medical costs. That funding will have to come from elsewhere—insurance, perhaps, or from your own pocket.

• **Little or no inherited assets.** The real danger is not that it may cost you your inheritance to pay for your parents' future care, but that it may cost you your retirement and/or your children's inheritance as well, because your parents ran out of assets. Some years ago, there were numerous studies showing that nearly $11 trillion will be passed down by the World War II generation to their offspring, the baby boomers. It was supposed to be the largest transfer of wealth in our country's history. Well, I've got news: it's not coming. Here's why. When those studies were done, the fact that the boomers' parents are living longer than anyone imagined was not taken into account. As they live longer and incur more expensive illnesses to treat, the World War II generation is annuitizing the inheritance it had intended to pass to its offspring and grandkids. Thus, if you are a boomer or younger, you will be looking to manage the stress that comes from trying to accomplish three equally demanding fiscal tasks: (1) supplementing your parents' care costs, (2) sending your own children through college, and (3) attempting to save for your own retirement and future care needs. Be prepared.

• **Care facility housing shortage.** At this writing, there are approximately 20,000 nursing homes in America. That's the good news. The bad news is that we need *one million* new beds a year, and as a country we haven't even begun to plan for how those units will be financed and constructed. Thus, as noted in the professional care conversation (see chapter 7), our parents (but even more so ourselves and our children) will be more and more compelled to consider (or reconsider) the financial and other aspects of alternative combinations of care, such as at-home medical care, at-home nonmedical care, at-home physical, respiratory, and even occupational therapy. And those are just the housing needs for end-of-life issues, not the transitional type of housing most seniors, especially of the baby boom generation, will initially need. The key to dealing with this is to anticipate it, not only by reviewing and updating your parents' care plan accordingly, but your own future care plan as well.

• **The impact of the microchip.** Computerization will continue to have a huge impact on dozens of fields associated with the parent care issue, from medicine, security, and communications to financial management. In the coming years, expect technology to play a much greater role than it does even now in how health care is both delivered and monitored in this country. Already, there are technologies that allow you to monitor your parents' care from your laptop with video and audio. Health-monitoring devices are available that transmit real-time health data across wireless networks from implanted devices or flashcards that hold a lifetime of medical records. There are already security companies using the power of the Internet and fiber-optic cable to allow parents to live independently longer, with heightened levels of protection and monitoring so that the slightest variation in a parent's normal pattern of behavior triggers a support team to go into action. As such developments become more widespread and commonplace, they will play an increasingly vital role in the design, updating, and rapid-response capability of any parent care plan.

❖ Keep in Mind!

The purpose of creating a parent care plan is to lower anxiety and increase confidence about the future for your aging parents and yourself. The continual review and updating of any plan is essential to sustaining that confidence in the future and not falling into crisis mode. Reduction in public levels of care support, more responsibility being placed on children to care for their parents, and increased reliance on technology all require that your parent care plan be updated to take into account the effects of these trends and your parents' naturally evolving circumstances on the original plan. Updating a parent care plan after its original design should be viewed much like seeing your doctor on an even more regular basis after you hit age fifty. It just makes sense.

An Act of Will

Caregiving is a duty, an honor, a burden, and frequently exhausting and irritating. It is, to borrow a line from Charles Dickens, "the best of times and the worst of times." It provides feelings of limitless joy and bottomless despair. It is walking to the car thinking how well your mom or dad looked one day, and walking away in tears on another, wishing, "If only this could end."

Caregiving is not for the fainthearted. It is not for the weak-minded. It is not for quitters—definitely not for quitters. Once you have agreed to do it, you must keep doing it no matter what. You must do it when your parent is aware of your presence and knows who you are, and you must do it when your parent hasn't a clue who you are and isn't even aware you are there.

You must do it when the weather is in your favor: bright sun, clear sky, and a soft breeze. And you must do it when the elements are snow, sleet, and freezing rain. You must do it when that voice in your head keeps saying it's OK to skip today because you would rather be doing something else—*anything else.* But you must persevere because, while many may start the caregiving project with you—brothers, sisters, friends—only a few will finish with you. So, caregiving is often not just about doing *your* job but the jobs of others as well. And you must do it when you feel appreciation for your efforts from all concerned, and when you feel totally taken for granted. At the beginning and at the end, caregiving may be act of love, but in the long middle, it is purely an act of will.

Caregiving is an act of generosity, and it is in that act of generosity that the dangers lurk, for in addition to money, generosity can deplete your stores of energy, love, dedication, and time. And when these resources dwindle, what will rush in to replace them is quite often resentment, bitterness, anger, and exhaustion. What I hope you will understand from this admonition is that I have been there. I have been and remain a fully participating member of the caregiving cast. That's why I created the parent care conversation strategy, to help transform the caregiving experience from that of an almost totally nightmarish situation if left to the last minute to a more positive experience—or at least as positive as possible—if addressed early on and strategically.

When I began conceiving this book, my father was entering his fourth year in the special care ward of Brighton Gardens, in

Charlotte, North Carolina. I remember him as not being able to button his shirt, wash his hair, or remember whether he had lunch or not. I would watch him struggle to line up his words with his thoughts so his sentences flowed from his mouth with the logic and in the order he wanted them to (but they seldom did). Watching this took its toll on me, though that toll was nothing compared to what he was going through. No matter how well designed a parent care plan may be, it cannot prepare you for, or prevent you from experiencing, things like that. It is a road map for care planning and caregiving, but not, unfortunately, an antidote for cancer, arthritis, Lou Gehrig's, Parkinson's, or Alzheimer's disease. It cannot place on hold the inevitabilities of getting older.

But what it can do is this. As I watched my father surrender to the disease that finally killed him, I was suddenly struck, not by how far he'd gone down but by how far I'd come up. The parent care experience had been thrust upon me; it had moved me from being an audience member in that drama called "My Aging Dad" to a supporting role on stage. The effect on my perspective was transformational. Among other things, I had gone from having no time for conversation with my dad about his future care and my role in that care to having loads of time for conversations with him, in which he could no longer participate due to Alzheimer's. My wish for you and your parents is that the parent care conversations will open the door to the same transforming experience, but one that will enable you and your aging parents to say the things to each other and do the things for each other that you've always put off. To do them *now*—and not wait for the memorial service, when it's too late.

ACKNOWLEDGMENTS

Acknowledgments in books like this are much like acceptance speeches at the Academy Awards: unless you were in the movie they are more often than not meaningless.

Nothing could be further from the truth in this particular "movie." In fact, none of this book could have been written without input, inspiration, and enthusiasm from the following:

Dan Sullivan and Babs Smith, partners and founders of The Strategic Coach Program, a lifetime focusing program for entrepreneurs that not only focused my life but transformed it.

Joy Tutela, Literary Agent Extraordinaire, with the David Black Literary Agency, New York, whose belief, persistence, and unrelenting determination to get this published was priceless.

John McCarty, my writing collaborator whose proposal crafting expertise made Joy's work easier and my relationship with Penguin possible and whose structure allowed me to write effortlessly.

Lee Pennington and Mark Bass of Lubbock, Texas—World-Class Financial Planners, World-Class Human Beings, and friends of mine when at times all my friends were them.

Scott Fischer of Fischer Capital—Money and Friendship do not often go together much less arrive simultaneously at the same point. His support in the past, his belief in the future, and his bottomless well of appreciation and enthusiasm for this project has been it's sustaining structure.

Brian Carroll, Tim Hodge, Susan Aldridge, Paula Abrams, my support team and cheerleaders in Charlotte, North Carolina.

Mark Patterson of Patterson-Thomas: Packaging, Branding, Visionary Design of Parent Care from the very beginning.

Marilyn, Julia, and Shannon Waller, who continue to provide an incredible example of family and who believe in me like a family should.

David Cashion, my editor at Penguin who showed up with not only a check for a first-time author but confidence, creativity, and collaboration as well.

The dogs: Katy, Roxanne, and Zack, whose morning walks keep me sane and whose company daily reminds me that loyalty, love, and caring are not just limited to humans.

Finally, Christine Sheffield and her daughter Ashley who have been my family for many years now and who invested unselfishly nearly five years of Saturdays, Sundays, and midweek days to make sure I could care for my father in the way that I was able to.

INDEX